POWER AND
PROSPERITY

POWER AND PROSPERITY

*Outgrowing Communist
and Capitalist Dictatorships*

Mancur Olson

BASIC
BOOKS

A Member of the Perseus Books Group

Designed by Rachel Hegarty

Library of Congress Cataloging-in-Publication Data
Olson, Mancur.
    Power and prosperity : outgrowing communist and capitalist
dictatorships / Mancur Olson.
        p.   cm.
    Includes bibliographical references and index.
    ISBN 0-465-05196-0
    1. Economic policy.   2. Comparative economics.   3. Free enterprise.
4. Post-communism.   I. Title.
HD87.O47 2000
338.9—dc21   99-052774
                                                            CIP

00 01 02 03 / 12 11 10 9 8 7 6 5 4 3 2 1

CONTENTS

FOREWORD

THE QUESTION OF HOW POWER RELATES to prosperity has occupied people's minds for centuries. Indeed, sometime around 1340, the leaders of the Italian city-republic of Siena commissioned a pair of frescoes that confront this question directly. Painted by Ambrogio Lorenzetti and dominating the room in which Siena's ruling Council of Nine deliberated, these two pictures are known as the *Allegory of Bad Government* and the *Allegory of Good Government*. The commissioned work presents an early and simplified view of the problems that Mancur Olson tackles in *Power and Prosperity*.

In the Lorenzetti frescoes, bad government, represented by the figure of Tyranny, sitting before a crumbling city wall, holds court over a series of vices: Cruelty, Treason, Fraud, Furor, Division, War, Avarice, Pride, and Vainglory. Scenes of various depredations, war, crime, and the trampling of justice surround the labeled figures, painted with all of the dramatic expression and costume apparently required of medieval public art. In contrast, on the wall to the right, a large figure of the Common Good presides over the effects of good government including Wisdom, Peace, Justice, Faith, Charity, Magnanimity, and Concord.[1] Notable among the figures in the *Allegory of Good Government* are two groups: a group of soldiers and prisoners and, to their left, a collection of councilors. These two subplots are of particular focus in Olson's book: the exercise of power and the role of citizenry in this process.

There are two scenes adjacent to the fresco of Good Government: the Good City and the Good Country. They display the prosperity that comes with successful governance arrangements. Harvesters dot bountiful fields in the Good Country fresco and donkeys easily carry bags of grain up the gentle hills. Their destination is the busy marketplace in the Good City fresco. Dancers and artisans, busy streets, and well-kept buildings round out the Good City. As helpful as the message may have been for the internal governance of Sienna, the regime that commissioned these paintings fell in 1355, undermined by the plague and following the approach of an external threat (Charles IV) and an uprising of local interests. Sienese development froze in time, preserving a city-sized museum of medieval life but also pointing out the frailty of lessons about good governance, even when displayed on the scale of a highway billboard.

Six hundred and thirty-six years after the painting of these frescoes, a reporter's questions prompted Mancur Olson to ponder why, after the collapse of a bad government, does prosperity not occur. Whereas Lorenzetti had an allegorical answer, Olson had a lifetime of pondering the sources of both public and private prosperity, along with training and innovation in the discipline of economics. This book is the result.

Olson identifies the conditions necessary for economic success: on the one hand, secure and well-defined rights for all to private property and impartial enforcement of contracts and, on the other hand, the absence of predation. He observes that these conditions occur most reliably, and thus with greatest economic effect, in rights-respecting democracies where institutions are structured in ways that give authoritative decision making to encompassing, rather than narrow, interests. Olson suggests that these arrangements describe the type of governments needed for growth. While there may be contract enforcement and systems of property in small groups or isolated markets, complex markets needed for growth cannot develop without government. Without the constraints provided by political institutions of democracy it is more difficult to develop credible systems of property or contract enforcement.

Olson explores this conclusion with particular respect to the Soviet Union and its successor states, but with applicability to the problems of many other places where prosperity remains elusive. With phrasing as vivid as Lorenzetti's frescoes, Olson looks behind the picture to ask why some governments provide public goods that support markets while others undermine prosperity.

While the contrast represented by the Lorenzetti frescoes concerns the outcome of governance, debate about postcommunism has often viewed the state and market as incompatible alternatives, not complements. While this view may be understandable as reaction to the historical antimarket role of the Soviet state, it does not, Olson notes, particularly help in understanding the necessary role of the state in places that have prospered.

The differences in the depth of the postcommunist economic collapse and the differences in the pace of recovery have much to do with the strength of the state and how the state uses its power. Levels of foreign and domestic investment, the growth of new private firms, and other measures of transition success depend on the state supplying basic institutions and forbearing from its own predation. If courts will not reliably enforce contracts or if their judgments are unenforceable, or if the state or its officials are necessary partners in private investment, then the state falls short. While this general point is easily made, Olson brings rigorous attention to the incentives of regimes and the specifics of how governance interacts with growth-affecting institutions.

After he wrote this manuscript, Olson coined a phrase that summarizes his answer of what type of government is needed to achieve prosperity. He suggested that a government powerful enough to create and protect private property rights and to enforce contracts, yet constrained so as to not, by its own actions, deprive individuals of these same rights, will be a *market-augmenting government*. The question of how to provide market-augmenting arrangements has broad applicability: from issues of the adequacies of courts and contract enforcement to the regularity of fiscal activities of government or access to education. The issues emphasized by Olson's phrase are relevant across a wide range of countries facing challenges today.

An area of economic activity that provides a particularly pointed example of the importance of market-augmenting government is the market for capital and credit. The sensitivity of these markets to institutions caught Olson's attention. In effect, he asked: Why is it when technology and institutions permit trillions of dollars to flow across borders that financial flows slow to a trickle within the borders of many countries? Certainly information about the structure of banks and banking regulation, about the operation of capital markets, is freely available and indeed subsidized to the poor countries of the world (donors spend billions of dollars supplying experts and training local officials in the details of capital and credit markets). As Olson noted to colleagues:

> In the most prosperous countries, the markets for capital, insurance, and derivatives, and for futures trading are so numerous and important—and capital intensive and large-scale corporate production is so extensive—that the government of these countries must generate more markets than they repress

or replace. The net effect of these governments is evidently to increase the extent of markets and the gains from trade. Why must it be government . . . ? Scholars of a libertarian bent have occasionally argued that contracts can be privately enforced. We know however in practice that private enforcement of property rights by competing enforcement agencies would lead to conflict. . . . Indeed an economy that relied on private enforcement may even lose the peaceful order that allows the existence of spot markets. . . . Prosperous economies need market-augmenting government.[2]

Pressing his insights against the specifics of the Indonesian, Korean, Thai, and Malaysian collapse in 1997 occupied Olson's last weeks. And while there have been volumes written about the events that triggered that financial collapse,[3] an important factor in the differences in the depth of the collapse and perhaps in the pace of recovery among these economies can surely be found in attention to the matters emphasized by Olson's market-augmenting government.[4]

Concluding that government plays an essential role in augmenting markets leaves us with a further challenge. Even if we can think more clearly about what it is that market-augmenting government does, how is it that you get more of it? In some respects, Olson's observation that rights-respecting democracies constrain predation and provide secure individual rights avoids the story of how you get a rights-respecting democracy in the first place. The variety of paths taken by now-successful countries provides less specific guidance for today's reformers than we might hope. At the same time, Olson often observed, the wide variety of examples of successful growth suggests that you can get lots of things wrong, or less than completely right, and still grow. But all of the places that grow consistently over long periods provide for the fundamentals emphasized by Olson. Thus, understanding the ways in which reforms can take place is an important challenge that lies mainly ahead.

Of course, one explanation for changes in institutions comes from considering the incentives of those in power. Much of Olson's effort in this book relates to the fiscal incentives of regimes to provide for better institutions for growth. He also explains the bounds that aging and succession place on the level of these incentives with respect to autocrats. Notwithstanding this qualification, the self-interest of governments is a partial answer to the question of how better institutions come about. To inform this self-interest, Olson's work here and elsewhere suggests that a necessary mechanism for change is to increase the understanding of elites, both inside and outside of government. Research, interactions, teaching, training, and publicizing ideas about the logic of institutions and collective choice are needed.

The opportunities for applying insights about the working of economic and political systems come at various times. In the upheaval represented by the collapse of the Soviet model, or the 1997–98 financial crisis of Asia (and in Indonesia, the succession crisis), there is great opportunity for addressing questions that do not expose themselves in the ordinary course. The effort to consolidate authority, in nominally democratic fashion, requires in the main an appeal to encompassing interests. These opportunities occur at times that Polish reformer Leszek Balcerowicz refers to as "moments of extraordinary politics."[5]

The problem of how better institutions came about is not uniquely one of developing or transition countries. Because even democracies will tend to favor narrow interests over broad ones (though less so than autocracies), Olson had a pessimistic view of the ordinary outcome of government. This was never the way he would have stated it, as he was so per-

sonally energetic and confident in the triumph of understanding. But he argued that most of us, even in democracies (and
particularly in stable democracies), are "rationally ignorant"
of many narrow policies to which our governments attend.[6]
He argued that long-stable societies come to suffer from narrow special interests. Absent revolution or other crisis, and
perhaps even in these circumstances, how is it that better institutions come about? No single answer exists, yet it seems
to me that challenge to debilitating arrangements occurs more
often in places with more open public debate and political
processes, better capability for independent research, and
greater exposure to the pressure of "crises" of new technology
or competition from foreign or related domestic markets.

It is my own experience, both in the United States and now
in many other countries, that good scientific knowledge about
the institutional basis for economic performance can play an
essential role—not that other political forces will lean over in
the face of reason, but that good research arms advocates, who,
absent such intellectual support, have only bad politics against
them. For example, in the United States the successful deregulation of transportation in the 1970s and 1980s can be attributed to information on economic costs and institutional
mechanisms that helped upend costly but well-protected policies.[7] In Nepal, simple facts about the costs of business licensing in time and bribes reduced licensing time from years to
days. Knowledge of the details of institutional design would
have been useful in posttransition Russia or postapartheid
South Africa. For example, the processes that have produced
the poorly functioning, asymmetric federal structure in Russia
have roots not only in the initial distribution of economic resources but in choices made with respect to constitutional design, privatization mechanisms, and electoral processes. Such

insight is immensely valuable in Indonesia today, and one day when China opens itself to debate, it may affect the well-being of a fifth of humanity. In this context, it was Olson's hope that this book and its different emphasis may play a useful role.

For places with more locked-in institutional arrangements, including both the persistently poor countries of Africa or South Asia and the sclerotic, though relatively rich, democracies, the opportunity for improved understanding, by itself, to make dramatic difference may be constrained.[8] But this simply emphasizes the great importance of increasing the information and analysis of these costs and of doing a much more creative job of communicating the results to both elites, and through them, popular political forces. But these are only observations. What are the advances in theory that remained for Olson and now remain for others? If the reader is a voter in a poor country finding its way, or an official in an advocacy group or a government official, what are the further questions to draw from this thinking? One measure of Olson's advance is that the following questions are increasingly the focus of debate in the post-Olson world.

How do transitions to more market-augmenting governance begin? Specifically, what occurs within the set of incentives for the regime?

If we knew more about the process of reform, would we think differently about the order of reform?

Are different market-augmenting institutions appropriate for countries at different levels of development?

What is the impact of regional or global integration of markets on the demand for better local institutions? When globalization proceeds, do better institutions become more or less important?

Which types of conflict or other stress affect certain institutions?

How useful are "grassroots" or local initiatives in the absence of attention to fundamental institutional arrangements at the national level?

What are the limits of self-regulation of private efforts to
promote market-augmenting services?

Readers will have their own set of issues and questions, as
well as points of disagreement, after reading this book. But
that is exactly as Olson would have wanted it.

> Many researchers have ... an instinct for the capillaries and
> there is some work in the journals that, even when it is right,
> is hardly worth bothering about. Just as the great fighter is
> looking for the jugular, so the great scientist is looking for ar-
> eas where there can be a breakthrough—for areas where strong
> claims are in order. Thus I think it is a good research strategy
> to search for stark and simplifying propositions. In my career I
> like to think that I have always done that. That is certainly the
> only thing that I want to do. (Mancur Olson)[9]

The stark idea in this book combines central topics in political science and economics: power and prosperity. While
most readers may not appreciate that the two disciplines
had for a long time downplayed the relationship between
power and prosperity, Olson continues in this book his life's
work of reestablishing political economy as a central intellectual concern for social scientists and policy advocates.
This reach is reflected in the wide attention to Olson's work
in fields beyond economics—political science and sociology
in particular.

Olson's research and writing took him in many directions,[10]
but he will be remembered by at least a generation of students

specifically for his work on the ability of individuals to organize for collective action and the provision of group goods—
ranging from goods used by members of a primitive village, to
higher wages for members of a union or better government
policies for citizens of a nation. His early and most-cited book,
The Logic of Collective Action,[11] explained why groups often
fail to act in their collective self-interest and how those that do
manage to succeed.[12] This insight, so completely incorporated
into our thinking today as to seem almost banal, forced re-
thinking of many assumptions common at the time. An early
classic in the field of public choice economics—or as Olson often tried to retitle it, "collective choice"—this work spawned
an industry of reaction, testing, and extension. Whole confer-
ences and courses were organized around these issues as other
scholars challenged the limits of Olson's theory and applied it
to different problems. The book itself has been translated into
nine languages. The durability of the essential insight of this
work is seen in the persistence of discussion about the ideas.

Twenty and thirty years after Olson's book, political scientist
Russell Hardin's *Collective Action* (1982) and economist Todd
Sandler's *Collective Action: Theory and Applications* (1992)[13]
capture ongoing evolution of the debates spawned by Olson's
1965 work. Almost two decades after *The Logic of Collective
Action*, Olson's extension of these ideas to the problems of national prosperity resulted in *The Rise and Decline of Nations:
Economic Growth, Stagflation and Social Rigidities*.[14] This
volume attracted immediate notice, in 1983 winning the
American Political Science Association's Gladys M. Kammerer
Award for the best book on national policy and many positive
reviews in the general circulation press. Translated into twelve
languages itself, this volume sweeps across economic history
to ask how the logic of collective action might explain the eco-

nomic growth and stagnation of various political jurisdictions. Among the advances on the earlier work is the idea that a broader *encompassing* interest group would advocate policies more closely aligned with the general interest than would a narrow special interest.

Although the provision of public goods by governments as countries grow was certainly relevant to Olson's examination of the evolution of successful Western market economies, Olson turned, in the mid-1980s, to the question of why poverty is so persistent in many countries. An early summation of his ideas about the problems of development in poor countries is in the 1987 "Diseconomies of Scale and Development."[15] Here Olson suggests that a major challenge of poor societies is not their lack of resources but rather their difficulty organizing large-scale activities, particularly governmental activities. Thus, simply importing large-scale governmental organization is not likely to be the path to more successful public goods production. "Whatever the optimal role of government may be in developed nations, it is smaller in developing countries."[16]

A later and more broadly ranging examination of the sources of persistent national poverty came in the 1996 "Big Bills Left on the Sidewalk: Why Some Nations Are Rich, and Others Poor."[17] Here he asks why the flow of ideas and people, as well as capital, does not lead to converging levels of income among nations. With a memorable phrase typical to his style of exposition, Olson draws on a story of an economist who, upon seeing a hundred-dollar bill on the sidewalk, explains that he is not bothering to pick it up because if it were real it would have already been picked up. We need, Olson argues, a better explanation of why poor countries appear to leave many bills on the sidewalk. He dismisses the idea that differences in resource endowments (especially human capital) or technology explain

persistent poverty. Rather institutions and economic policies—attributes that are mainly defined by national boundaries—affect the ability of the poor and others to pick up their
own big bills. The best thing a country can do is "wise up," he
concludes. And this wising up depends very much on economists doing a better job explaining how the structure of incentives affects growth. It is wrong, Olson suggests, simply to
expect that political bargaining will lead to the best of all
worlds.[18] The examples of stubborn poverty around the globe,
as well as theory, contradict this view. This idea is advanced in
Chapters 3 and 4 of the present volume.

While others debated whether government was a part of the
problem or a part of the solution, Olson's effort had long
turned to the more useful issue of what kind of government,
what kind of arrangements of government, led to economic
growth. What constitutes "wising up"? This inquiry had two
main concerns: What types of services do governments provide to promote growth? And what types of governments provide these more consistently? These inquiries of course led to
the current book and to Olson's coining of *market-augmenting government*. Those who have read some of Olson's work
in the professional literature of the last decade,[19] or who have
heard him speak, will recognize the trail of several pieces in
the present volume. Measures of institutional development
utilized in some of that work have become standard in the
profession for studying the relationship of governance and various outcomes.

Olson died suddenly in 1998 before he had put the final
touches on this book. Fortunately, he had completed a pol-
ished draft of arguments both fresh and important, though
not yet, in the author's view, fully honed. Are the arguments
put forth in *Power and Prosperity* stark and simplifying as

the quote above suggests Olson always wanted? I believe the answer, even if readers debate the logic, is an unqualified yes. Though this book is unfinished, there can be no doubt that in it Olson continues his pursuit of the breakthrough idea.

He had received many comments on the ideas presented in this book and in his last months one of his central activities was to respond to critics and thus strengthen both his argument and his exposition. In 1996 and 1997, two very helpful seminars on these ideas were organized by the Luxembourg Institute for European and International Studies. Two different groups of experts from disciplines in addition to economics—history, political science, sociology, and others—convened in Washington and in Bourglinster, Luxembourg, to debate the broad ideas, as well as the details of this book. The institute, as it has with other important books, will shortly publish that conversation. It will be an interesting complement to this book. Those comments, as well as many lengthy correspondences Olson received directly, suggest that these are difficult issues and that whatever one's view of Olson's capillary description, he is onto a jugular issue. Among the many research projects truncated by his unanticipated and tragic demise were several inquiries extending the insights, and testing the ideas in this book, many prompted by reactions to the drafts of this writing. Because these efforts were not yet completed to Olson's satisfaction, this book, like any that makes such a broad argument, will still leave some issues unaddressed. This volume is thus offered as Olson's last symphony, no less enjoyable or important on account of his desire to make yet more improvements.

This book tackles subjects of importance. Faced with a world experiencing dramatic political and economic change, Olson was searching for explanations not only for specific developments but for the underlying logic that explained why examples of more successful societies are but a short plane ride or television broadcast away.

The central role that Olson assigned to the search for logic does not imply that he was after some ivory-tower theory. Political leaders, scholars, and outsiders who would provide advice all benefit from having an incisive theory of how development occurs. Olson worked and wrote for all of us. In a comment that was either a criticism of the work of some colleagues, or perhaps instead a rebuttal to sponsors who objected to funding research rather than mechanically applied technical assistance, Olson remarked that the "best theory is intensely practical." In this volume, Olson reaches for a theory that explains fundamental functions of government and at the same time leads to steps that can improve on the usual outcomes.

This confidence that a better theory was needed and that such a line of inquiry would have immense and immediate utility is what led Olson to focus in his last decade on establishing the Center on Institutional Reform and the Informal Sector at the University of Maryland. Here he could himself apply the stark and simplifying ideas to immediate problems. This initiative also brought colleagues at Maryland and from around the world to press scholarship more closely to the knotty problems of governance and growth.

Mancur Olson left the project of his life suddenly and uncompleted. This book is but one manifestation of that; the truncated conversations and debates with scores of colleagues around the world are another measure. The nineteen briefcases he left behind, each containing separate projects of varying vintage, are yet another. This book will, like much that Olson did, provoke debate and further inquiry. As others have noted, Olson's style was to relish such challenges. He took every questioner, and most questions, seriously. For those of us so fortunate as to have worked with him, we can almost call up the questions he would pose in return to our points. Yet this is more likely evocative of his distinctive style; it does not provide the specific genius and the energy that would make interaction with Mancur so enjoyable and challenging.

Among the unfinished aspects of this book was a dedication. But it is clear from material Mancur left, as well as conversations with his wife Alison, that he would have dedicated this volume to his three children: Ellika, Severin, and Sander. So I conclude by conveying this dedication.

Charles Cadwell
College Park, Maryland
September 1999[20]

PREFACE

THE TELEPHONE RANG on the evening of August 19, 1991, the first day of the Soviet hard-liners' putsch against Mikhail Gorbachev. I was sadly watching the television reports, which were saying that the putsch seemed to be successful. The telephone call was from a favorite columnist who asked some shocking questions. Wasn't the only hope for the stalled Soviet economy, he asked, a no-nonsense dictatorship that would impose a free-market regime on the Soviet Union? Hadn't the economic performance of Chile under the pro-market dictatorship of Ugarte Pinochet, of South Korea under Chung Hee Park and Doo-Hwan Chun, of Taiwan under Chiang Kai-shek and his son, of Singapore under Lee, and of mainland China under Xiaoping Deng brought rapid economic growth? Hadn't I shown, in *The Rise and Decline of Nations* (1982), that the lobbies and cartels that accumulate in democratic societies eventually rob them of their dynamism? Hadn't Soviet economic performance, as leaders of the Soviet putsch claimed, plummeted as Gorbachev introduced his somewhat democratic reforms and let the Soviet satellites go their own ways?

Though the conversation went on until my wife had called me for dinner twice, I did not provide the shocking answers that the columnist was hoping to obtain. The problem was not so much that I was hesitant about supplying an instant analysis of such momentous and complex issues—I had, as it happened, been thinking about these issues for some time. The problem was that I did not know the answers.

The questions would not leave me, in part because they related to my daily work. Just months before the columnist's call, I had become involved in an effort to research and provide advice on economic policy and institutional reforms to formerly communist and third-world countries. At the University of Maryland, I established a Center on Institutional Reform and the Informal Sector (IRIS), which was at first funded exclusively by the U.S. Agency for International Development. IRIS has since had offices or programs in forty-five formerly communist or third world countries, and in many of these countries there were sometimes questions disturbingly similar to those the columnist had posed. Some Indians, for example, told people from IRIS that they wondered whether India's economy had not fallen behind those of China, Singapore, Taiwan, and South Korea because India was a democracy. An erudite Russian, then in the Russian government, told me in Moscow that he feared that Russia's democratic revolution would soon reach the "Thermidor" phase in which it devoured its own. When I naively pointed out that it was shortly after Thermidor that Napoléon set up his dictatorship and engaged in aggression throughout Europe, he replied, as though to a child who knew nothing of the harsh ways of the world, "Of course!" When the analogies were not to the French Revolution, they were to Weimar Germany. I was left thinking about what would happen if a Napoléon or a Hitler came to control Russia's nuclear stockpiles.

This sort of experience concentrates the mind and as a result—thanks in large part to a flow of information from many countries and to fresh research from colleagues—the columnist's questions could be answered. The biggest problem had been the lack of an appropriate intellectual framework. Nowhere in the literature was there a systematic understanding or satisfactory theory that encompassed both dictatorship and democracy, much less the market as well. Luckily the insights that were needed to achieve a systematic understanding gradually emerged. With them, it was no trick to work out the intellectual framework or theory that was needed to deal with the columnist's questions.

Then it seemed that serendipity knew no bounds. As an economist, I could easily combine the new framework with standard economic theory to present solutions for how to make a country's economy thrive. Take, for example, the question of how a society obtains the kind of market economy that generates high and continually increasing incomes. Even in the poorer third world countries, markets are everywhere. Within hours of leaving the airport, the visitor to a third world country encounters any number of peddlers and merchants. There are bazaars filled with astute traders and the typical village has its shops, markets, or market days. Yet the economies work badly and the people are poor. After the collapse of communism, markets become ubiquitous. In Moscow, just after the freeing of prices at the beginning of 1992, people were trading at virtually every Metro stop and kiosks appeared on almost every sidewalk. Even two generations of communism had not eliminated the entrepreneurial spirit, so countless markets emerged spontaneously. Yet at the same time the people were poor and production was falling not only in Russia but in many other formerly communist countries as well.

What is it that makes some market economies rich whereas others are poor? What policies and institutions does a country need to change from a market economy of peddlers and bazaars to a market economy that generates a cornucopia of riches? In developing the theory that answers the columnist's questions, this book also provides a large part of the answer to the seemingly very different question of why there are innumerable markets in almost every society, yet riches in only a few.

With these answers, we can quickly understand why there were dramatically different outcomes after the defeat of fascism and after the collapse of communism. At the end of World War II, most observers expected that West Germany, Japan, and Italy would remain in poverty for quite some time. The United States was concerned that it might for many years need to provide much of the food needed to keep the populations of these societies alive. In fact, all three of the defeated Axis nations enjoyed rapid economic growth as soon as the constraints of the war and occupation had been removed. These three episodes of growth were so far beyond explanation with the prevailing theories that they were called "economic miracles." By contrast, when communism collapsed, the people who had endured the economic absurdities of Soviet-type economic systems, like most Western observers, expected that economic performance would improve dramatically. In fact, in many of the formerly communist societies economic performance so far has been even worse than it was under communism. Every formerly communist country suffered from a drop in output, if not a collapse, and many are taking a very long time to recover. Though I believe that the official statistics in the ex-communist countries exaggerate the drop in real incomes and I am personally optimistic about the future of some of these economies, there can be no doubt that economic performance has been below expectations.

The extraordinary and unexpected difference between economic performance after the defeat of the Axis powers and after the collapse of communism is all the more remarkable in view of the desires of the victorious countries in World War II. For some time after World War II, the victorious countries were fearful that Germany and Japan would again emerge as aggressive dictatorships, so they did not want them to develop strong industrial economies or even to become unified countries. By contrast, the countries that were the winners in the cold war from the outset wanted to help the once-communist countries develop successful societies in the image of the West. Thus, one question this book asks is: Why was economic performance so much better, especially in relation to expectations, after the defeat of fascism than after the collapse of communism?

The lifting of the iron curtain revealed something else that the developed nations of the West, whether they had been winners or losers in World War II, did not expect to see: an extraordinary amount of official corruption and Mafia-style crime. In Russia, for example, some polls indicate that crime and corruption are considered the most significant problem of the society. Though there are, of course, corrupt officials and Mafia organizations in most Western countries (and in major American cities there is probably more street crime than in the formerly communist countries), the extent of official corruption and organized crime in the ex-communist countries (and especially in the former Soviet Union) is outside the range of Western experience. Therefore, another question this book asks is: Why do the formerly communist countries suffer so much from official corruption and organized crime?

The reason that this book is able to answer the foregoing questions is that, after the intellectual framework that was needed to deal with the columnist's questions was available and was combined with standard economics, we have an intellectual structure that simultaneously encompasses both markets and governments. Whether societies are rich or poor, they obviously have both economies and polities. The economies move the polities and the polities govern the economies. Therefore, theories of markets that leave out government—or conceptions of politics in which the economy is exogenous—are inherently limited and unbalanced.

They do not tell us much about the relationships between the form of government and the fortunes of the economy or adequately explain why some societies are rich and others are poor.

Though Adam Smith, John Stuart Mill, and some other great economists in prior centuries included government and politics as well as firms and markets in their analyses, economists in the twentieth century have not, until rather recently, recovered this grand ambition. The first great twentieth-century economist to do this was Joseph Schumpeter, with his inspiring and brilliant (but not prescient) book on *Capitalism, Socialism and Democracy*. In an acknowledgment of this contribution, I titled early versions of this book *Capitalism, Socialism and Dictatorship*. However, the current title, *Power and Prosperity*, was chosen to communicate the main idea more clearly. Robert Klitgaard thought of the subtitle *Outgrowing Communist and Capitalist Dictatorships*. For this I am most grateful not only because of the dual meaning of the word *outgrow* but because it reminds us that even the most secure and developed democracies want more impressive economic growth than the world's dictatorships (after adjusting for their higher starting points and lesser catch-up potential). The argument in this book, if correct, has important implications for economic policy in advanced democracies of Europe, North America, and Japan, as well as in the countries that are or have lately been under dictatorships.

I have made strong claims in this Preface. It is not for me, but for reviewers, readers, and the authors of subsequent studies, to judge whether these claims are true. If my claims are not true, I deserve severe criticism. Though I have built upon the work of others and have had an extraordinary amount of invaluable information, help, and criticism from colleagues, and especially those at IRIS and the Department of Economics at the University of Maryland, I am solely responsible for all of the shortcomings in this book as well as for any unwarranted claims. If the reader studies all of the pages that follow, I shall be grateful, however severe the standard by which they may be judged.

Mancur Olson

POWER AND
PROSPERITY

1

THE LOGIC OF POWER

THESE DAYS, VIRTUALLY ALL ECONOMISTS (and I think also most people in other fields) would agree that societies are most likely to prosper when there are clear incentives to produce and to reap the gains from social cooperation through specialization and trade. If a society is to achieve its highest possible income, the incentives must not only be clear but must induce firms and individuals in the economy to interact in a socially efficient way. That is, they must be similar to the incentives in perfectly competitive industries: those where the market, in addition to having other virtues, is so large—or the firms in it are so small—that no single firm has a monopoly power or a perceptible effect on price.

When we shift from what is best for prosperity to what is worst, the consensus would probably be that when there is a stronger incentive to take than to make—more gain from predation than from productive and mutually advantageous activities—societies fall to the bottom. In a Hobbesian anarchy, where there is no restraint on individuals' incentives to take things from one another, or in a kleptocracy, where those in power seize most assets for themselves, there is not much production or many gains from social cooperation through specialization and trade.

What determines where a society falls between the one extreme, where each firm and individual has an incentive to do what would best serve the welfare of the population, and the other, where predation eliminates investment, specialization, and trade? What determines whether there is a pattern of incentives that generates efficient production and social cooperation, or one that yields nothing more than subsistence? We need to find out what those in power have an incentive to do and why they obtained power. When will those with power in a society have an incentive to use their power to promote production and social cooperation? When will they take much of the gains from production and trade? And why did those who have power obtain it? To begin to answer these questions, we need to understand the logic of power.

A theory of power has long been the Holy Grail for political science, but the Grail has not been found. Some economists have tried to deal with power by extending the market model: they begin with the voluntary transaction—the Coaseian bargain—and then use the transaction costs that limit trade and bargaining as the basis of a theory of government and politics. Some of these economists go on to extend the Coase theorem—the idea that, unless transaction costs are too great, individuals have an incentive to bargain until they have maximized their joint gains—to government and politics. This extension leads these economists to believe that power tends to be used in socially efficient ways. I explain this intriguing belief—and show that it is vitiated by a logical error that has previously been overlooked—in Chapter 3. But it should be immediately evident that the logic of power cannot be adequately explained through voluntary transactions: power—and not least governmental power—is the capacity to bring about compulsory compliance, and thus it involves compelling authority and the capacity to coerce. As we shall see, it is not enough to understand the theory of voluntary exchange: we must also understand the logic of force.

The Criminal Metaphor

Power is exercised by human beings, who are, of course, extraordinarily complex. As I see it, human beings rarely act out of unmixed motives. There is not only self-interest but also a benevolent element—and even a malevolent streak—in human nature. Historical outcomes surely depend not only on the incentives and self-interest of those with power but also on their morals and temperaments. I will, before the end of this book, analyze some contexts where disinterested and principled choices are decisive for progress of societies, but I start with a focus on the incentives and inducements to rational and self-interested action that face those with power.

For our focus on coercive power and our analysis of self-interested behavior, I use a criminal metaphor. Clearly, we cannot understand robbery as either a voluntary trade or a moral act, and thus it helps us to focus only on the self-interested use of coercive power. With the aid of this metaphor, we will be able to see beneath the surface and then construct the needed theory. Since criminal behavior is the exception rather than the rule in a successful society, the criminal metaphor will also remind us of the extent to which we are abstracting from the complexity of human nature.

Consider the incentives facing the individual criminal in a populous society. Other things being equal, a criminal is better off in a rich society than in a poor society: there is more to steal. Theft also makes societies less prosperous than they would otherwise be—the time devoted to theft produces nothing, but it reduces the rewards from productive work and investment and induces a diversion of resources from production into guards, locks, police, prisons, inventory control systems, and the like. Therefore, the crime committed by each criminal reduces the wealth of society and thus also the amount that is available to steal. Does this make the individual criminal curtail his or her crime?

Everyone already knows that it does not, but we must understand why. The typical individual thief in a society of, say, a million people, bears about one-millionth of the loss to society that occurs because his crime makes society's output less than it would otherwise be. Yet he alone normally bears the whole loss of whatever opportunities for theft he passes up. Therefore, the gain to criminals from a wealthier society and the reduction in that society's wealth due to crime do not keep crime from paying. (The opposite would be true only in a bizarre case where the loss to society from a theft were about a million times or more as valuable as what was taken by theft.) It is only society's punishment of criminals that keeps crime from paying, and it is not always sufficient to inflict punishment. Though each criminal has a stake in the prosperity of society, that stake is so minuscule that the criminal ignores it: he normally takes everything there is in any purse or till. As we shall see, it makes a huge difference whether individuals with coercive capacities have a minuscule or *narrow* stake in the society, on the one hand, or an *encompassing* interest, on the other.

Before turning to encompassing interests, we must remind ourselves that the same self-interest that made the criminal steal leads to dramatically different results when there is voluntary exchange in the market. If, say, better deterrence of crime led our criminal to serve his interests through voluntary exchange in the labor market, he would typically take the job that offered the highest pay. No profit-maximizing employer employs a worker who does not add at least as much to the firm's revenues as that worker costs. In self-interestedly seeking the highest wage, our ex-criminal works at jobs where his marginal social productivity or contribution to output tends to be greatest.[1]

Now let us contrast the individual criminal in a populous community with the head of a Mafia family or other criminal gang that can monopolize crime in a neighborhood. Suppose that in some well-defined turf, a criminal gang cannot only steal more or less as it pleases but can prevent anyone else from committing crime there. Obviously, the Mafia family has an incentive to keep other thieves out of its own domain. But will it gain from taking all that it can on its own ground? Definitely not.

If business in this domain is made unprofitable by theft, or migration away from the neighborhood is prompted by crime, then the neighborhood will not generate as much income and there will not be as much to steal. Indeed, the Mafia family with a true and continuing monopoly on crime in a neighborhood will not commit any robberies at all. If it monopolizes crime in the neighborhood, it will gain from promoting business profitability and safe residential life there. Thus, the secure Mafia family will maximize its take by selling protection—both against the crime it would commit itself (if not paid) as well as that which would be committed by others (if it did not keep out other criminals). Other things being equal, the better the community is as an environment for business and for living, the more the protection racket will bring in. Accordingly, if one Mafia family has the power to monopolize crime, there is little or no crime (apart from the protection racket). The considerable literature on monopolized crime makes it clear that secure monopolization of crime does, in fact, usually lead to protection rackets rather than ordinary crime. Outbreaks of theft and violence in Mafia-type environments are normally a sign that the controlling gang is losing its monopoly.[2]

This criminal metaphor illustrates the theory of narrow and encompassing interests presented in my book *The Rise and Decline of Nations*.[3] The individual robber in a populous society obtains such a narrow or minute share of any loss or gain to society that he ignores the damage his thievery does to society. By contrast, the Mafia family that monopolizes crime in a community has, because of this monopoly, a moderately encompassing interest or stake in the income of that community, so it takes the interest of the community into account in using its coercive power. Whereas the individual criminal in a populous society bears only a minuscule share of the social loss from his crime, the gang with a secure monopoly on crime in a neighborhood obtains a significant fraction of the total income of the community from its protection tax theft. Because of the encompassing interest in the income of society that this monopoly gives, it bears a significant fraction of social losses, including those from its own protection tax theft. Therefore, though the individual criminal normally takes all of the money in the wallet he steals, the secure and rational Mafia leader never sets a protection tax rate anywhere near 100 percent: this would reduce the neighborhood's income so much that the Mafia family itself would be a net loser.

The Stationary Bandit

A story about a Chinese warlord suggests that we need to take this logic further.[4] In the 1920s, China was in large part under the control of various warlords. They were men who led armed bands with which they conquered a territory and then appointed themselves lords of the territories they had conquered. They taxed their subjects heavily and used the proceeds to serve their own interests. The warlord who I was reading about, Feng Yu-hsiang, was noted for the exceptional extent to which he used his army for suppressing thievery and for his defeat of the relatively substantial army of a notorious roving bandit called White Wolf. Apparently, most people in Feng's domain wanted him to stay as warlord and greatly preferred him to the roving bandits.

At first, this situation was puzzling: Why should warlords who were simply stationary bandits continuously stealing from a given group of victims be preferred, by those victims, to roving bandits who soon departed? The warlords had no claim to legitimacy and their thefts were distinguished from those of roving bandits only because they took the form of relentless tax theft rather than occasional plunder.

There is a good reason for this preference. As we have seen, there is little production in an anarchy and thus not much to steal. If the leader of a roving bandit gang who finds only slim pickings is strong enough to take hold of a given territory and to keep other bandits out, he can monopolize crime in that area—he becomes a stationary bandit. The advantage of this monopoly over crime is not mainly that he can take what others might have stolen: it is rather that it gives him an encompassing interest in the territory akin to that of the Mafia family considered in the previous section. He actually has a stronger encompassing interest than the Mafia family, since the bandit leader who takes over an anarchic area does not have competition from any government's tax collectors: he is the only one who is able to tax or steal in the domain in question.

This monopoly of theft changes incentives dramatically. We have seen that the individual criminal in a populous society has such a narrow or minuscule interest in the society that he rationally ignores the damage he does to it, which is obviously also true of a gang of bandits passing through. These socially perverse incentives make anarchies work badly. The encompassing interest of a stationary bandit leader who can continue to keep out not only other criminals but outside tax collectors as well gives him an incentive to behave very differently.

First, it leads him to reduce the percentage he takes from each victim of his theft. As we have seen, the criminal who is only one among many will take 100 percent of the money in any till he robs. By contrast, the stationary bandit with continuing control of an area wants to make sure that the victims have a motive to produce and to engage in mutually advantageous trade. The more income the victims of theft generate, the more there is to take. A secure stationary bandit, by making his theft a predictable tax that takes only a part of his victims' outputs, thereby leaves them with an incentive to generate income. If he cuts his rate of tax theft from 95 percent to 90 percent, he doubles his subjects' posttax reward for production and trade, which might well increase output and tax receipts by a large multiple.[5]

The stationary bandit keeps on gaining from reducing his rate of tax theft down to the point where what he gains (from tax theft on a larger output) is just offset by what he loses (from taking a smaller share of that output). He is left at the revenue-maximizing rate of tax theft.[6] If the stationary bandit cut his tax rate from 51 percent to 50 percent, thereby raising output of his domain from 98 percent to 100 percent, he would essentially maximize his tax collections: he would receive half of the increase in output, which would be approximately offset by the reduction in his share of total output. That is, the stationary bandit, because of his monopoly on crime and taxation,[7] has an encompassing interest in his domain that makes him limit his predations because he bears a substantial share of the social losses resulting from these predations. If the stationary bandit in the example above increases his tax rate from 50 percent, he bears about half of the social or "deadweight" loss from the distortion of incentives that this higher rate of predation brings about, which is enough to keep him from taking more. Generally speaking, the greater the loss in production from taxation at any given rate of tax, the lower the rate of tax theft at which the stationary bandit's take is maximized.[8] Though the deadweight losses and how they vary with tax rates—and thus a stationary bandit's rate of tax vary from case to case—every stationary bandit has a rate of tax theft that is always lower than 100 percent—and usually much lower—which maximizes his collections.

A Benefactor to Those He Robs

The second way in which the encompassing interest of the stationary bandit changes his incentives is that it gives him an incentive to provide public goods that benefit his domain and those from whom his tax theft is taken. Paradoxically, he provides these public goods with money that he fully controls and could spend entirely on himself. We know that a public good benefits everyone in some area or group and that many public goods, such as levees that protect against floods, police that deter crime, and quarantines that limit contagious diseases, make a society more productive.

Because the stationary bandit obtains a known share of any increase in the output of his domain, given by his optimal rate of tax theft,[9] he has an incentive to spend his resources on all productivity-enhancing public goods up to the point where his last dollar spent on these goods equals his share of the resulting increase in output.[10] Thus, if the stationary bandit's optimal rate of tax theft is 50 percent, he will spend on public goods up to the point where the last dollar spent on these goods adds $2 to the output of the domain, since he will then receive $1. More generally, if the stationary bandit's share of any increase in output is S, he will best serve his interests by spending the resources he controls on public goods up to the point where the output of the domain increases by $1/S$. Readers who want formal proofs and a mathematical and geometric exposition of this argument should consult an article by Martin McGuire and myself on "The Economics of Autocracy and Majority Rule."[11]

The Origin of Autocracy

In short, the bandit leader, if he is strong enough to hold a territory securely and monopolize theft there, has an encompassing interest in his domain. This encompassing interest leads him to limit and regularize the rate of his theft and to spend some of the resources that he controls on public goods that benefit his victims no less than himself. Since the settled bandit's victims are for him a source of tax payments, he prohibits the murder or maiming of his subjects. Because stealing by his subjects, and the theft-averting behavior that it generates, reduces total income, the bandit does not allow theft by anyone but himself. He serves his interests by spending some of the resources that he controls to deter crime among his subjects and to provide other public goods. A bandit leader with sufficient strength to control and hold a territory has an incentive to settle down, to wear a crown, and to become a public good– providing autocrat.

Thus, governments for large groups of people have normally arisen because of the rational self-interest of those who can organize the greatest capacity for violence. These violent entrepreneurs naturally do not call themselves bandits, but on the contrary give themselves and their descendants exalted titles. They sometimes even claim to rule by divine right. Since history is written by the winners, the origins of ruling dynasties are, of course, conventionally explained in terms of lofty motives rather than by self-interest. Autocrats of all kinds usually claim that their subjects want them to rule and thereby nourish the usually false assumption that their governments arose out of some kind of voluntary choice.

Once we understand how the incentives of a bandit gang change when it can settle down and securely hold a territory, we see why the warlord's subjects, even though he extracts tax theft from them year after year, prefer him to the roving bandits who rob only sporadically. Roving banditry means anarchy, and replacing anarchy with government brings about a considerable increase in output. The subjects of a stationary bandit obtain the proportion of the increase in income that is not taken in taxes. The logic of the matter—and historical information and recent observations—suggests that the continuing exactions of a stationary bandit are far better than anarchy.

It follows that the familiar metaphor of the predatory state is inadequate, even for autocracies with utterly selfish leaders. As we saw earlier, a stationary bandit has an encompassing interest in the territory he controls and accordingly provides domestic order and other public goods. Thus, he is not like the wolf that preys on the elk, but more like the rancher who makes sure that his cattle are protected and given water. No metaphor or model of even the autocratic state can therefore be correct unless it takes account of the stationary bandit's incentive to provide public goods while maximizing his rate of tax theft.

The Historical Record

From history, we know that the encompassing interest of self-interested autocrats can be consistent with economic growth and even the advance of civilization. Autocracy has been commonplace at least since King Sargon's conquests created the empire of Akkad in ancient Mesopotamia not long after the first development of settled agriculture. Most of humanity over most of history has been subjected to autocracy and exploited by tax theft. It is very difficult to find examples of benevolent despots. The stationary bandit model fits the facts far better than the hypothesis that autocrats are altruistic.

Yet, remarkably, there was considerable growth of total income, population, and civilization in the age before democracies came to be dominant. There has also been rapid economic growth in more recent times under several autocracies. Admittedly, I shall argue later that relatively democratic societies—or at least nonautocratic societies with representative governments—have played a disproportionate role in economic progress,[12] which is no accident. But it is obviously impossible to explain the growth under extravagant and self-interested autocrats without taking account of their encompassing interests.

The Other Invisible Hand

Though the shift from roving to stationary banditry brings gains to both the bandit leader and the population, it does not arise by social contract or any other voluntary transaction. It is not the result of the invisible hand that often makes voluntary market transactions serve a social interest. Yet the increase in output and the mutual gain that arises when a roving bandit leader settles down and appoints himself king are the result of a response to incentives: the surprisingly good results under my stationary bandit model owe nothing to good intentions.

Thus, the improvement in outcomes that arises when there is a shift from the destructive to the constructive use of power—as when Hobbes's "war of all against all" is replaced by the order provided by an autocratic government—is due to another invisible hand. This invisible hand—shall we call it the invisible hand on the left?—that guides encompassing interests to use their power, at least to some degree,[13] in accord with the social interest, even when serving the public good, was not part of the intention. This second invisible hand is as unfamiliar and perhaps counterintuitive as the first hidden hand was in Adam Smith's time, but that does not mean it is less important. There can be no satisfactory theory of power, of government and politics, or of the good and the harm done by governments to economies, that leaves out the second invisible hand.

Princely Consumption

At first, it might seem that the cost of the consumption of an autocrat, even if it should be lavish, is trivial in relation to the tax revenues of a country. Our introspection may suggest that an autocrat will be able to buy everything she could want with a minute percentage of tax receipts, so she would not, as the logic in this chapter predicts, extract as much surplus as she could from the society. Here our introspection is inapt because we have (unless we are autocrats ourselves) bourgeois conceptions of consumption. The costs of Imelda Marcos's 3,000 pairs of shoes and other extravagances added up, and the Pyramids, the palace of Versailles, and the Taj Mahal cost even more. The autocrat's country may also be a stage for his ego: Fidel Castro's "mind darted here and there, as new ideas occurred to him. He encountered a bridge and ordered it fixed. His jeep bogged down, and he said 'Pave the road.' Drought hit an area of the island and he ordered a new dam. At once."[14]

For an autocrat, keeping up with the Joneses means keeping up with other kings or dictators, which often means not only fabulously expensive, prestigious projects but also the armies and wars that may obtain a more imposing domain. It took a huge part of the national incomes of Germany and the Soviet Union to satisfy the tastes of Hitler and Stalin.

Thus, there is substantial evidence of autocrats who spent so much to realize their goals that, even though they took as much in taxes as they could, they ended up short. We see this pattern even in some of the largest autocracies in the history of the West. The Roman Empire was taxed until it was destroyed. The Hapsburgs in Spain collected all the taxes they could yet incurred (and sometimes repudiated) large debts. The Bourbons in France did the same and their regime ended because of a fiscal crisis. The Soviet Union's taxation, as we shall see later, was implicit but uniquely high, yet in the end the Soviet system also could not find the resources needed to keep its government going.

Comparing Autocrats and Majorities

The model of autocracy that has just been set out shows that a secure autocrat's encompassing interest in the society makes him limit the extent of his tax theft. Though the autocrat's encompassing interest implies that he will use some of the resources he controls to provide public goods that increase the productivity of his domain, he does this only to maximize the absolute amount of his net extraction from society. The gains from autocracy therefore come at a high price—a large redistribution of income from the subjects to the autocrat.

How do democracies compare, in this respect, with autocracies? Different representative governments have different structures and procedures, which change outcomes to a degree. The easiest way to understand how democracies differ redistributionally from autocracies is to start with the simplest democracy in which there are two candidates for a presidency or two well-disciplined parties seeking to form a government run entirely in the interest of the winning majority. This starting assumption is, as we shall see, somewhat too favorable to representative government because it implies that a society is governed by a more encompassing interest than it would have if it were governed by changing coalitions of small parties, each representing only a small part of the income-earning capacity of the society; or if it were governed under the influence of special interests representing only a particular industry, occupation, or other narrow interest. I shall deal with the influence of narrow interests on democracies later.

Throughout I avoid giving democracy an unfair advantage by assuming no better motivation than under autocracy. For the sake of impartiality as well as parsimony, then, I assume that democratic political leaders are just as self-interested as autocrats and seek to win by opportunistically obtaining majority support.

The Electoral Incentive for Efficiency

Observation of two party democracies tells us that incumbents like to run on a "you never had it so good" record. An incumbent obviously would not leave himself with such a record if, like the self-interested autocrat, he took for himself the largest possible net surplus from the society, and we do not observe this happening in democracies. But we are too favorable to democracy if we assume that the incumbent party or president will maximize his chances of reelection simply by making the electorate as a whole as well off as possible.

A candidate needs only a majority to win, and he might be able to "buy" a majority by transferring income from the population at large to a prospective majority. The taxes needed for this transfer would impair incentives and reduce society's output just as an autocrat's redistribution to himself does. Would this competition to buy votes generate as much distortion of incentives through taxation as a rational autocracy does? That is, would a vote-buying democratic leader, like the rational autocrat, have an incentive to push tax rates to the revenue-maximizing level?

Though both the majority and the autocrat have an encompassing interest in the society because they control tax collections, the majority additionally earns a significant share of the market income of the society, which gives it a more encompassing interest in the society's productivity. The majority's interest in its market earnings induces it to redistribute less to itself than an autocrat redistributes to himself. This situation is evident after considering an option that a democratic majority has if it is at the revenue-maximizing tax rate. A minuscule change in tax rate will not alter tax collections. A minuscule increase will reduce the national income so that even though a larger percentage of income is taken in taxes, the amount collected remains unchanged. A minuscule reduction in the tax rate will increase national income sufficiently that, even though a smaller percentage is taken, tax receipts are unchanged. This is the optimal tax rate for the autocrat because changes in the national income affect his income only by changing tax collections.

But a majority at the revenue-maximizing tax rate is bound to increase its income from a reduction in tax rates: when the national income goes up, it not only collects taxes on a larger national income but it also earns more income in the market. So the optimal tax rate for the majority is bound to be lower than the autocrat's. The easiest arithmetic example comes from supposing that the revenue-maximizing tax rate is one-third and that the majority earns one-third of the national income in the marketplace. The rational autocrat will then find that the last dollar in taxes that he collects reduces the national income by $3, and one-third of this loss is his loss, so he breaks even on this last dollar of tax collection and is at his revenue-maximizing rate. But if a majority mistakenly chooses this same tax rate, it hurts itself, for it loses $2 (the same dollar lost by the autocrat, plus $1 of market income) from the last dollar it collected in taxes. Thus, a majority would maximize its total income with a lower tax rate and a smaller redistribution to itself than would be chosen by an autocrat. Readers who want formal proof of this proposition and various collateral results can find them in the previously cited article on "The Economics of Autocracy and Majority Rule."

The Reciprocal Rule

More generally, it pays a ruling interest, whether an autocrat, a majority, or whatever, to stop redistributing income to itself when the national income falls by the reciprocal of the share of the national income it receives. If the revenue-maximizing tax rate were one-half, an autocrat would stop increasing taxes when the national income fell by $2 from his last dollar of tax collection. A majority that, say, earned three-fifths of the national income in the market and found it optimal to transfer one-fifth of the national income to itself, would necessarily be reducing the national income by five-fourths, or $1.25, from the last dollar that it redistributed. Thus, the more encompassing an interest—the larger the share of the national income it receives taking all sources together—the less the social losses from its redistributions to itself.

The same reciprocal rule determines how much a ruling interest spends on public goods. We saw that an autocrat gained from spending on public goods up to the point where the last dollar spent on public goods increased the national income by the reciprocal of his tax rate. The autocrat's tax rate, of course, determines his share of the benefits. The share of the benefits of public goods received by a ruling interest that earns income in the marketplace is necessarily larger: it is given by the part of the society's income that it redistributes to itself plus the fraction of market income that it receives. A redistributive ruling interest that earns income in the market will continue spending on public goods until the last dollar it spends increases the national income by the reciprocal of its share of that national income. The hypothetical redistributive majority in the previous paragraph that earned three-fifths of market income and transferred one-fifth of the society's income to itself would gain from spending its money on public goods up to the point where the national income went up by five-fourths of a dollar. Just as a more encompassing interest redistributes less to itself, so it also spends more of its resources on public goods that benefit the whole society.

Note that the same reciprocal rule governs both the point at which a ruling interest ceases to gain from redistributing to itself and also how much of its money it pays to spend on public goods. This reciprocal rule applies to all types of regimes, whether autocratic or democratic.[15]

Though the argument above mentions only majorities, it applies to any ruling interest that earns some of its income in the market at the same time that it controls the government, whether this ruling interest is less or more than a majority. The income the ruling interest earns in the market, when added to the interest it has in the productivity of the society because (like the autocrat) it controls the fisc, necessarily gives it a more encompassing interest than an autocrat would have. Therefore, it will bear a larger share of the social losses resulting from redistribution to itself and will also obtain a larger share of the benefits of public goods.

Similarly, a ruling interest that represents a larger fraction of the income-earning capacity of the society will (because it necessarily has a more encompassing interest in the society than a ruling interest representing a smaller fraction of this capacity) redistribute less income to itself and provide more public goods than a ruling interest that represents a smaller fraction of the income-earning capacity of the society. If, for example, a democracy such as the United States or Switzerland has checks and balances that imply more than a majority is normally required for major policy changes, then the ruling supermajority will redistribute even less income to itself and will provide an even larger supply of public goods than a majority representing a smaller fraction of the society's income-earning capacity.

Superencompassing Majorities

Astonishingly, sometimes majorities and especially super-majorities have a sufficiently encompassing interest in society that they will, out of pure self-interest, forgo redistribution to themselves and treat the minority as well as they treat themselves. They will provide the same amount of public goods as would be provided if the society unanimously agreed on the Pareto-efficient or socially ideal level of provision. Whenever there is a superencompassing interest, the second invisible hand—the one that guides encompassing interests in the use of coercive power—works in complete accord with the interest of all. In this circumstance, the second invisible hand, like the first invisible hand in a perfect market, works with Pareto-efficiency,[16] and even those with a capacity to take whatever they please, take nothing.

Though these conclusions initially seem to run against all intuition and common sense, upon closer examination there is a simple and straightforward resolution of the paradox. The surprising result grows out of the combined effect of the two cutting forces in the theory of narrow and encompassing interests.

The first cutting force is the relationship between the breadth of the stake in a society or domain and the extent to which it pays to take from it. We have seen that the individual criminal in a populous society bears only a minute share of the loss his depredations impose on society, so he takes no account of them. We have seen that the Mafia family takes some account of the harm its depredations do, that the autocrat curtails his rate of tax theft to a greater degree because of this harm, and that the ruling interest that also earns income in the market restricts redistributions to itself even more. Moreover, we recall that, as the share of market income earned by a ruling interest goes up, it gains from redistributing less to itself. This declining tendency to take as an interest becomes more encompassing is due to the incentive-distorting effects of taxation and theft. Though in economics we sometimes find it useful for some theoretical purposes to imagine a lump-sum tax—one that, simply by assumption, has no effect on incentives—all continuing taxes in the real world affect incentives,[17] and there are even many cases where the social losses from taxes are a multiple of the amount collected from the tax.

It follows that, as we consider majorities that earn higher and higher percentages of the income of the society, we necessarily reach a point where the majority bears so much of the social loss from redistribution that it necessarily loses from it. This situation is true even if the social loss from redistribution is untypically small; if a redistributive tax reduces society's income by only 2 percent, a ruling interest that obtains, say, 99 percent of income, would still lose from imposing this tax. Even if the social loss were less than 2 percent, there would have to be a point before the encompassing interest would become synonymous with the whole society, where it would lose from imposing a redistributive tax.

The great practical significance of this logic becomes evident when we combine it with the second cutting force—the second blade of the scissors—in the theory presented here: the incentive that encompassing interests have to provide public goods.[18] We saw that a stationary bandit has an incentive to provide public goods out of resources that he controls and could spend on himself, up to the point where his share of the marginal social benefit from the goods equals their marginal cost, so an autocrat with an optimal tax rate of 50 percent would spend on public goods until his half of the benefit from them equals the cost to him of providing more. If a majority that earns income in the marketplace replaces the autocrat, it obtains a larger part of the benefits of public goods and supplies more. The larger the fraction of earned income that a ruling interest receives, the more public goods it should supply in its own best interest; a higher tax rate is subsequently needed to defray the cost of these public goods.

The more encompassing interest, which gives a majority the incentive to tax more to provide a public good, comes up against the first blade of the scissors: it bears a larger share of the deadweight losses from taxation. Since a redistributive tax must be added on to the taxes needed to finance public goods, it necessarily brings a larger deadweight loss. As we saw, there necessarily must be an interest short of 100 percent of society that loses from redistributive taxation, even when there is no taxation to finance public goods. Since taxes are needed to finance public goods, and the amount an interest wants to spend on public goods goes up as it becomes more encompassing, *it follows that there are superencompassing interests that do not comprise all of society (and thus have a minority that they could exploit) that would lose from redistributing income from the minority to themselves.* The two blades of the scissors must come together and cut off the incentive to redistribute for interests that are less than the whole of society and have a minority that they could exploit.

If there is no incentive for the ruling interest to redistribute to itself, it will also try to have tax rates that coordinate the burden of paying for public goods with the benefits received from them. Thus, superencompassing interests, though totally self-interested, will also provide the same amount of public goods that they would have provided had they instead had a totally benevolent concern for the efficiency of the society. In all respects they treat the minority as well as they treat themselves. Those who want formal proof of these propositions can find them in the aforementioned "Economics of Autocracy and Majority Rule."

Though there is no presumption that most majorities are superencompassing, some of them definitely are. With the help of a graduate assistant at IRIS, Tom Bozzo, the computer was programmed to calculate whether a redistribution to a ruling interest would be optimal for a ruling interest that obtained a specified fraction of the society's market income, for each of a gigantic number of tax-distortion functions. This procedure was repeated for each of a large number of other specified fractions of market income that different ruling interests could earn. The results of these simulations made it clear that superencompassing ruling interests are a feature of many real-world situations and are perhaps not at all rare.

Suppose that it is in the interest of a majority to spend a fourth of the gross domestic product (GDP) on public goods and that any extra tax collections beyond those necessary to raise the funds for these public goods would reduce the national income by a third more than they bring in. Then an interest that earned more than three-fourths of the national income could not gain from redistributing income to itself. Checks and balances and explicit more-than-majority requirements for certain crucial decisions are common in democratic political systems, so bare majorities often cannot get their way, which makes superencompassing interests show up more often in many democracies. Moreover, as William Niskanen pointed out when extending an earlier version of my argument, even bare majorities that represent those of median income and above represent much more than half of a society's income-earning capacity.[19] Such majorities are surely sometimes superencompassing.

The Other Dimension

We have now examined the logic of power for interests so narrow that they take no account of the interests of society and for interests with such an encompassing stake that their self-interest leads them to act as though they were totally benevolent. We have also seen that these are the polar extremes of a continuum and that the results at different points depend on how close the interest with the power is to the one extreme or the other.

In this analysis I have taken it for granted that each interest has an incentive to think of the long run (i.e., what economists refer to as a Barro infinite planning horizon). So long as each interest has a fairly long-term stake, all of the foregoing results hold to an approximation.

In reality, some interests have no reason to be concerned about the long run. For very narrow interests, this makes no difference: they take little or no account of the interests of society whether they are thinking of the long run or the short run. But for encompassing interests, it makes a great deal of difference.

There is also a time continuum, and as the planning horizon of an interest with power becomes sufficiently short, it takes no account (no matter how encompassing its interest may be) of the interest of society. The next chapter discusses the profound importance of time dimensions, especially with relevance to our understanding of the economic performance of autocracies and democracies.

2

TIME, TAKINGS, AND INDIVIDUAL RIGHTS

JUST AS THERE IS A GREAT GAIN to an anarchic society when the leader of a roving bandit gang has the power to seize and securely hold a territory and make himself an autocrat, a vast loss to society results from the opposite shift. To understand this important loss, we must first consider the gains to society—and to secure autocrats—that arise from long-term investment.

We know that an economy will generate its maximum income only if there is a high rate of investment and that much of the return on long-term investments is received long after the investments are made. Thus, an autocrat who is taking a long-term view will try to convince his subjects that their capital will be permanently protected not only from theft by others but from confiscation by the autocrat himself; if his subjects fear expropriation, they will invest less, and in the long run his tax collections will be reduced.

To reach the maximum income attainable at a given tax rate, a society must enforce contracts (including those involving long-term loans) impartially, but the full gains are again reaped only in the long run. To obtain the full advantage from long-run contracts, a country also needs a stable currency. A stationary bandit will therefore reap the maximum harvest in taxes—and his subjects will get the largest gains from his encompassing interest in the productivity of his domain—only if he is taking an indefinitely long-term view, and only if his subjects have total confidence that their rights to private property and impartial contract enforcement will be permanently respected and that the coin or currency will retain its full value.

Suppose that an autocrat is only concerned about getting through a short period such as a year. He will then gain from expropriating any convenient capital asset whose tax yield over the year is less than its total value.[1] He will also gain from forgetting about the enforcement of long-term contracts and from repudiating his debts, as well as from coining or printing new money that he can spend even though this ultimately brings inflation.

At the limit, when an autocrat has no reason to consider the future output of society, his incentives are those of a roving bandit, which is, in effect, what he becomes.[2] Therefore, just as a surprising proportion of the progress of humanity is due to the incentive for roving bandit leaders to settle down and become rulers, so much of the confiscation and retrogression in human history is due to the incentive that autocrats, no matter how exalted their lineages or titles might be, often have to revert to what is essentially roving banditry.

Since an autocrat, no matter how secure and forward-looking he may be, can suffer reverses or other changes that give him a short time horizon, the subjects in an autocracy always face some risk that their capital will be confiscated, their loans repudiated, or their coin or currency debased. This risk reduces the amount of saving and investment even when there are secure and forward-looking autocrats. To be sure, the rational autocrat has an incentive, because of his interest in increasing the investment and trade of his subjects, to promise that he will never in any way confiscate wealth. But the promise of an autocrat is not enforceable by an independent judiciary or any other independent source of power—by definition autocrats can overrule all other power sources. Due to this situation and the obvious possibility that a dictator could come to take a short-term view, the promises of an autocrat are never completely credible. Thus, the model of the rational self-interested autocrat offered in the last chapter is too sanguine about economic performance under secure autocrats; it implicitly assumes that they will always have—and that their subjects believe that they will always have—indefinitely long planning horizons.

In fact, in any society with autocratic governments, an autocrat with the same incentives as a roving bandit is bound to appear sooner or later. And, as we should expect, the examples of confiscations, repudiated loans, debased coinages, and inflated currencies perpetrated by monarchs and dictators over the course of history are almost beyond counting.

"Long Live the King"

A ruler with absolute power cannot create an independent authority within the society with the power to ensure an appropriate or orderly succession: any independent authority with sufficient power to install a new ruler can remove the present ruler. Thus, it is inherent even in the definition of absolute autocracy that there is a special danger of succession crises.[3] As is evident from so many recent dictatorships in Africa and Latin America, for example, autocracies are extremely susceptible to succession crises and uncertainty about the future. Perhaps the most interesting evidence about the importance of a monarch's time horizon comes from the historical concern about the longevity of monarchs and from the once widespread belief in the social desirability of dynasties. There are many ways to wish a king well, but the king's subjects, as the foregoing argument shows, have more reason to be sincere when they say, "Long live the king." If the king anticipates and values dynastic succession, that further lengthens the planning horizon and is good for his subjects.

The historical prevalence of dynastic succession, in spite of the near-zero probability that the oldest son of a king is the most talented person for the job, probably owes something to an intuitive sense that everyone in a domain, including the present ruler, gains when rulers have a reason to take a long-term view. In an absolutist regime, it may be advantageous to all concerned if a consensus emerges about who the next ruler will probably be. This not only reduces the likelihood of a battle over succession but also increases confidence and thus investment, income, and tax receipts even in the present. Given autocracy, then, dynastic succession can be socially desirable, both because it may reduce the likelihood of succession crises and because it may give monarchs more concern for the long run and the productivity of their societies.

How Does Banditry End?

We have seen that, even though the second invisible hand gives the autocrat who expects a long rule a surprising incentive to be concerned about the productivity of his domain, he nonetheless maximizes the net surplus that he can extract from society for his own purposes. Worse still, whenever an autocrat has a sufficiently short time horizon, it is in his interest to confiscate the property of his subjects, to abrogate any contracts he has signed in borrowing money from them, and to use the mint or the printing press to obtain money for himself even though this debases the coinage or currency. Thus, it is natural, in spite of many historical advances under stationary banditry, that an autocrat's subjects prefer to keep his surplus for themselves, and that they want a greater security of property and contract rights than can be provided by a system that reverts to roving banditry.

Accordingly, even if we were to leave the ethical appeal of democracy and the moral abhorrence of banditry aside, we should still ask how autocracies come to be replaced by other systems of government. Autocrats often lose their jobs. They are turned out when officers of their armies organize a coup d'état, or when they are killed by a palace guard, done in when economic mismanagement leaves them without the resources to pay their retainers, or buried because they die of natural causes. So each autocrat's tenure ends—some end soon—and many of the endings come with a crisis of succession. But each autocrat is most often succeeded by another stationary or roving bandit: it is only in special circumstances that the end of an autocrat's reign leads to democracy.

What special circumstances explain the exceptional cases where a democratic—or at least a representative or non-autocratic—government replaces an autocracy? Since some nonautocratic, representative, and relatively democratic governments emerged well before the age of the universal voting rights, our focus should be on whether a government is a representative government chosen through free political competition for votes, not on whether it has a universal adult franchise.

We should at this point think of democracy, as Joseph Schumpeter did,[4] as a system in which the leadership of the present government is subject to replacement because of the free electoral competition of an alternative party or group. Though the breadth of the franchise is crucial for answering some other questions, it is not the key to the process whereby autocracies are replaced by representative governments. Modern history suggests that there is an overwhelming tendency for representative governments with limited franchises to evolve into the universal adult franchise, but this process has a different logic than the one that is at issue now.

One special circumstance that can account for a transition to democratic government is outside influence or even the forceful imposition of such a government from the outside. Imposition of democracy has occurred, for example, when democracies have defeated dictatorships in war. The richest and most technically advanced countries are and have for some time been mostly democracies, and democracies have more often than not prevailed in military competitions with autocracies.[5] In West Germany, Japan, and Italy after World War II, the victorious democracies imposed democratic institutions on the vanquished peoples, and these peoples, with vivid memories of the catastrophic consequences for them of their recent autocratic regimes, readily accepted democratic institutions. Outside pressure and influence also account for a number of other democratic governments.

The Autonomous Emergence of Democracy

It is difficult to find the special circumstances that explain transitions to representative government that are internal and spontaneous. Though it would be easy to argue that those countries that arrived at democracy autonomously were blessed with democratic cultures or selfless leaders, it would be evasive for me to explain the emergence of democracy that way here. Since I assume the self-interested behavior suggested by the criminal metaphor when analyzing autocrats, I should not rely on the ad hoc introduction of nobler motivations to explain the origins of democracies. I must instead endeavor to explain autonomous transitions to democracy by extending the parsimonious theory that I use to explain autocracy.

The theory suggests that a crucial condition for the autonomous emergence of democracy is the absence of the commonplace conditions that generate autocracy. The task is to explain why a leader who organized or helped to organize the overthrow of an autocrat would not make himself the next dictator. We have seen that autocracy is a most profitable occupation. The authors of most coups and rebellions have appointed themselves dictators. Thus, the theory here predicts that democracy would be most likely to emerge spontaneously when none of the individuals or group leaders who helped bring about the overthrow of an autocracy could make themselves autocrats.

We can therefore deduce that autocracy is prevented and democracy is permitted by the accidents of history that leave a balance of power among a small number of leaders, groups, or families—that is, by a broadly equal dispersion of power that makes it imprudent for any leader or group to attempt to overpower the others. This deduction by itself does not, however, give us an original conclusion: it rather points toward one of the major inductive findings in some of the literature in history and in political science on the emergence of democracy. If the theory here is right, there must be a considerable element of truth in the well-known Whig interpretation of British history and in the explanations of democracy offered by political scientists such as Robert Dahl and Tatu Vanhanen.[6] The historical and inductive literature suggests that the autonomous emergence of representative democracy in Britain, the United States, and elsewhere was associated with a pluralistic dispersion of power.

It is nonetheless necessary to go back again to the logic of the theory to find two further necessary conditions for the autonomous emergence of representative government. Even when there is a balance of power that keeps any one leader from assuming total control of a territory, that leader may be able to establish himself as an autocrat of a small domain. A dispersion of power and resources over a large area can result in a set of small-scale autocracies and no democracy. If, however, the different contending groups are scrambled together over a wide domain, then small autocracies also are not practicable. Therefore, a second necessary condition for the spontaneous emergence of democracy is that the different forces among which there is a rough balance of power should not be separated in a way that makes miniautocracies feasible.[7]

The third necessary condition is that the area in which democratic arrangements are emerging is spared conquest by neighboring regimes, whether because of geographical barriers, city walls, or other lucky circumstances.[8] In Chapter 1, we see that an autocrat collects more—and often a lot more—from taxpayers than he spends on public goods. It follows that, other things being equal, the bigger an autocrat's domain and the more taxpaying subjects he has, the greater his surplus. Thus, as William Niskanen pointed out in commenting on an earlier version of the present argument, autocrats have an incentive to expand their domains through aggression.[9] Democracies with a tendency to extend suffrage over the whole of their territories do not have this incentive.

The Logic of Power Sharing

Suppose there is a balance of power among different forces so that no leader can obtain dictatorial power and that the additional necessary conditions for the emergence of nonautocratic government are also satisfied. What then is the best possible outcome for each leader? Clearly it is better to share power than to have no power or influence. Thus, a leader who cannot become an autocrat has an incentive to cooperate with others in establishing a nonautocratic government. If different groups are mixed together and not confined to a single territory, their leaders may not have complete control over them. The best option for these leaders is to establish a representative government through which, as representatives of the groups they lead, they share power. No one can be certain in advance how elections will turn out, yet each group can, by allying with other groups, ensure that no other group will continually dominate elections. Elections as well as consensual agreements among leaders can be consistent with the interest of the leaders and members of each group. Thus government that is at least nonautocratic and probably also representative arises autonomously when there is a balance of power among different forces, and the other necessary conditions set out above also hold.

Though a small hunter-gatherer band may be able to make all significant decisions by consensus and have no need for a full-time governor, the situation is different when each leader represents a substantial number of people. Then the maintenance of a peaceful order and the provision of other public goods requires a formal government with some kind of hierarchy of officials to produce the needed public goods. The governmental hierarchy must have the power to compel citizens to pay taxes. It obviously must also have enough power to keep the peace. Since there is usually a need for military power to deal with other countries, a government's chief executive will normally be in charge of an army as well as a body of law enforcement officials.

Any government—and especially any new government— therefore necessarily gives its leader some advantages that can facilitate schemes that leader may devise to become an autocrat. Because democratic opponents may be extremely irksome and because the autocrat's role is extraordinarily rewarding, more than a few leaders of representative governments have taken advantage of opportunities to assume the role of president-for-life or some other autocratic title. Many representative governments have also been taken over by autocrats who started in other roles, such as being leaders in a country's armed forces. Thus, many power-sharing arrangements do not survive as representative governments.

The Logic of Limits on Power

Remember the incentives that led the small group of leaders to share power in the first place. A balance of power kept the leaders from becoming autocrats themselves. Each leader has an incentive to minimize the probability that an alternative candidate for the autocrat's role will become an autocrat! This is not only because a political competitor who achieves power might want to destroy his principal rivals but also because it is desirable to avoid being a victim of autocratic extraction. Thus the leaders who organize a representative government have an incentive to structure and limit this government in a way that will reduce the likelihood that its head becomes a dictator. Given the power that is inherent in the role of chief executive of a government, the devices that are used to prevent the emergence of autocracy do not always work, but those who agree to share power have strong incentives to make them work, so they sometimes do. Remarkably, then, the same conditions that give rise to the autonomous emergence of representative or democratic government also lead to structures and procedures that limit the power of the government and especially of the government's chief executive.

Representative Governments Institute Property and Contract Rights

When a peaceful order has been established in a society, most of those in it can best serve their interests by production and mutually advantageous trade. To produce efficiently, they need arrangements that delineate and protect property rights. To obtain the gains from those mutually advantageous trades that require third-party enforcement, the individuals in the society need to establish arrangements for the enforcement of contracts. Thus, mechanisms for defining and protecting property rights, enforcing contracts, and resolving disputes are in the common interest. Those who establish and maintain a representative government will therefore have an interest in some system to enforce agreements and resolve agreements—in a court system.

If these courts and the judiciary are under the control of the government's chief executive officer, they can be used, along with the other powers of government, to augment the power of the government leader. If those who adjudicate disputes about the ownership of property must do the bidding of the government leader, then that leader can claim any property she wishes. If those who oppose the head of the government can be punished at his command, then an autocracy is likely to emerge. There are similar but less serious problems if less powerful political officials control the courts.

Therefore, those who establish a power-sharing arrangement have an incentive to arrange for disputes about property and contracts—and about the interpretation of the law—to be settled by those who have no personal stake or interest in the dispute. If individuals have no such stake, they are likely to decide matters in accord with their beliefs about what is right—that is, in accord with their moral principles and the law—they have no reason to do anything else. It is, accordingly, in the interest of those who arrange for power sharing to work out social contrivances, like the jury and the independent judiciary, which can obtain the disinterested decisions that are needed. Long experience suggests that these social arrangements can work at least tolerably well. This is an aspect of life where ethical principles and groups' norms are decisive (and therefore one which I emphasize principle and not self-interested motivation).

Note that the same structures created by those in a power-sharing arrangement to ensure that they do not become victims of autocratic extraction also protect property and contract rights. In a true autocracy, by definition, there can be no power above that of the autocrat, and thus no mechanism that can ensure that subjects' property is not confiscated by the autocrat. By contrast, the very logic of the power sharing that creates a representative government generates such mechanisms.

Glorious Revolutions

Many transitions from autocracy to democracy have not been autonomous. Representative governments that emerged in the twentieth century and even in the nineteenth century owed something to the example—and sometimes also to the influence and power—of representative governments in the United Kingdom and the United States, and sometimes to other democracies as well. The democracy established by the U.S. Constitution was influenced by the political settlement in Britain in the Glorious Revolution of 1688–89, as were the democracies created in what were once the self-governing dominions of the British Empire.

Accordingly, the focus here is on the emergence of a genuinely representative government in Britain with the Glorious Revolution and on the establishment of the U.S. Constitution a century later. Though they have not survived continuously to the present day—and we have much less information about them—autonomous representative governments also emerged, for example, in Venice, Florence, Genoa, and some other city-states in northern Italy and in the Athenian and Roman Republics. For the most part, I shall leave the question of whether they support or contradict the present theory to others.

Happily, the initial emergence of representative government in England fits very nicely with the logic of the democratic transition that is predicted by the present theory. The civil wars in mid-seventeenth-century Britain produced no lasting winner. The different denominations and tendencies in British Protestantism and the economic and social forces with which they were linked were more or less evenly matched. There had been a lot of costly fighting and, certainly after Cromwell, no one with the power to defeat all of the others. The restored Stuart kings might have been able to do this, but their many mistakes, and the choices that ultimately united almost all of the conflicting Protestant political tendencies against them, finally led to their defeat.

None of the victorious leaders, groups, or tendencies was then strong enough to impose its will upon all of the others or to create a new autocracy: as the foregoing logic suggests, representative and relatively democratic government emerged in part because it was ultimately not feasible for anyone to make himself an absolutist monarch. As this logic also predicts, the leaders who made the Glorious Revolution had an incentive to design a power-sharing arrangement that reduced the probability that someone else would come to have absolute power over them. The best option available to each of the leaders or groups with power was to agree upon the ascendancy of a parliament that represented them all and to restrict the powers given to the government and the limited monarchs that they installed. The separate leaders and groups who made the Glorious Revolution also gained from taking out insurance against the autocratic power of others through an independent judiciary, a Bill of Rights, and an enhanced deference to the common law.

With a carefully constrained monarchy, an independent judiciary, a more secure common law, and a Bill of Rights, people in England in due course came to have a relatively high degree of confidence that any contracts they entered into would be impartially enforced and that private property rights, even for critics of the government, were relatively secure. In keeping with the logic of the matter, we see that the same arrangements and structures that reduced the danger that those who made the new arrangement would later become victims of a new autocracy also increased the security of property rights and the reliability of contract enforcement. Individual rights to property and contract enforcement were probably more secure in Britain after 1689 than anywhere else, and it was in Britain, not very long after the Glorious Revolution, that the Industrial Revolution began.

Though the emergence of a democratic national government in the United States was partly due to the example or influence of Great Britain, it was also due to the absence of a single group or colony capable of suppressing others. The thirteen colonies were all different, even on such matters as slavery and religion. The separate colonies had, in general, experienced a considerable degree of internal democracy under British rule and contained different religious and economic groups. The authors of the U.S. Constitution were, of course, also taken with the importance of a dispersion of power and checks and balances that would prevent autocracy. They were not least concerned to have courts and a judiciary that was not under the control of a king or president. Again, in keeping with the reasoning discussed earlier, the checks and balances, the independence of the courts, and the broad array of individual rights protected by the Bill of Rights not only minimized the likelihood of a tyranny but also protected property and contract rights.

Limited Executives and Stronger Property Rights

Though less is known (at least to me) about the northern Italian city-states, there is certainly no lack of examples of the operation of the same logic. Sometimes, when leading families or merchants organized a government for their city, they not only provided for some power sharing through voting but took pains to reduce the probability that the government's chief executive could assume autocratic power. For a time in Genoa, for example, the chief administrator of the government had to be an outsider—and thus someone with no membership in any of the powerful families in the city. Moreover, he was constrained to a fixed term of office, forced to leave the city after the end of this term, and forbidden from marrying into any of the local families.[10] In Venice, after a doge who attempted to make himself autocrat was beheaded for his offense, subsequent doges were followed in official processions by a sword-bearing symbolic executioner as a reminder of the punishment intended for any leader who attempted to assume dictatorial power.[11] As the theory predicts, the same city-states also tended to have more elaborate courts, contracts, and property rights than most of the European kingdoms of that time. As is well known, these city-states also created the most advanced economies in Europe, not to mention the culture of the Renaissance.

Large accumulations of inventories and capital goods in cities are especially difficult to protect from confiscation, and those with large fortunes are conspicuous targets for forced loans and other forms of autocratic extortion. The supply of capital in cities is also sensitive to the risk-adjusted returns in ways that the supply of land and other natural resources is not. Thus, autocratic confiscations and extortion should disproportionally reduce—and good property and contract rights should especially encourage—the growth of cities. It is significant that, as DeLong and Shleifer have shown, the cities of medieval and early modern Europe that were not under autocratic control grew much more than cities subjected to absolutist autocracy.[12]

Lasting Democracy Implies Lasting Property and Contract Rights

Though those who set up a representative government have an incentive to structure it in a way that limits the power of its leader and the probability that he will make himself an autocrat, they may not be successful. As we have noted, the chief executive officer of a government must have some powers that increase his capacity to become an autocrat. If those who set up a representative government go too far in restraining the executive, they can also leave the government incapable of fast action, making it more susceptible to defeat and takeover by foreign or domestic enemies. Thus, democracies often end through mistake or misfortune.

The establishment of a democracy and the conduct of an election does not necessarily bring secure contract or property rights. The individual rights that a democracy provides cannot be secure if the democracy itself is not. Property and contract rights in an insecure democracy may be abridged by an elected official on his way to autocratic power. They may also be negated by confiscations of capital, debasements of currency, or expropriations of unpopular minorities that the leadership of a fragile democracy may devise in trying to survive. There is, accordingly, no inherent connection between the creation of a democracy—or the holding of one or even a few elections—and the security of individual rights, including property and contract rights.

By contrast, there is a most profound and crucial connection between a lasting democracy or representative government and the property and contract rights important for economic progress. This connection is inherent in the logical conditions needed for democracy to survive. Obviously, a democracy is not viable if the rule of law is not followed when it calls for the current administration to leave office. A democracy also cannot survive if the opponents of the current administration do not have free speech and full rights under the rule of law, including property and contract rights. If even opponents of the administration in power must have these rights, then other citizens will also have them.

Property rights are simply individual rights that involve things that may be bought and sold. As James Madison aptly stated, "Just as a man may be said to have a right to his property, so he has a property in his rights."[13] Thus, the same court system, independent judiciary, and respect for law and individual rights that are needed for a lasting democracy also imply some secure property and contract rights.

As the foregoing reasoning suggests, the only societies where individual rights to property and contract are confidently expected to last across generations are the securely democratic societies. In an autocracy, the autocrat often has a short time horizon, and the absence of an independent power to assure an orderly legal succession means that there is always substantial uncertainty about what will happen when the current autocrat is gone. History does not provide even a single example of a long and uninterrupted sequence of absolute rulers who respected the property and contract-enforcement rights of their subjects. Admittedly, the terms, tenures, and time horizons of democratic political leaders are perhaps even shorter than those of the typical autocrat, and democracies lose a good deal of efficiency because of this. But in the secure democracy with predictable succession of power under the rule of law, the adjudication and enforcement of individual rights is not similarly short-sighted. Many individuals in the secure democracies confidently make even very long-term contracts, or establish trusts for great-grandchildren, or create foundations that they expect will last indefinitely, and thereby reveal that they expect their legal rights are secure for the indefinite future.

Statistical work that some of my colleagues at IRIS and I have done on all countries for which there is the needed data shows that there is a strong relationship between the length of time a democratic system has lasted and the security of property and contract rights in a society.[14] We also found that, in autocracies, the longer the tenure of an individual autocrat, the better the property and contract rights. Both of these results are completely in accord with the theory that has been offered here.

Not surprisingly, then, capital often flees from countries with continuing or episodic dictatorships, even when capital has great scarcity value in these countries, to the stable democracies, even though the latter countries are already relatively well supplied with capital and thus offer only modest rates of return. Similarly, the gains from contract-intensive activities such as banking, insurance, and capital markets are mainly reaped by stable democracies, for example, the United States, the United Kingdom, and Switzerland. Though experience shows that relatively poor countries can grow extraordinarily rapidly when they have a strong dictator who happens to have unusually good economic policies, such growth lasts only for the ruling span of one or two dictators. Thus, we should not be surprised that almost all of the countries that have enjoyed good economic performance across generations are countries that have stable democratic governments.

3

COASEIAN BARGAINS, TRANSACTIONS COSTS, AND ANARCHY

L ATER IN THE BOOK we shall greatly enlarge the theory that has been set forth in Chapters 1 and 2. Yet it is not too early to ask: What warnings should accompany the theory that has been set forth so far? And what is the best alternative theory? The best explanations are those that explain the most with the least, and that is what the two prior chapters have tried to do. The theory (as it should be) is simple. But reality is bewilderingly complex, and there is always the danger that this complexity is not recognized. We must, for example, recall the precautionary reason for the criminal metaphor. This metaphor was introduced partly to underline the point that we were considering only the self-interested use of power: by using the example of bandits, we not only abstracted from the richness and variety of human nature but did so conspicuously. Thus, we are reminded, for example, that there cannot be only stationary bandits but perhaps also benevolent despots.

By applying the assumption of pure self-interest impartially to majorities and other ruling interests no less than to autocrats, it is possible to compare the implications of the encompassing interests of an autocrat with the more encompassing interests of a majority, and thus to be certain that the better results under majorities did not arise from sneaking in (or unconsciously making) an assumption about nobler behavior. The discovery that there are sometimes majorities and other ruling interests with a superencompassing stake in society, so they treat minorities as well as they treat themselves and supply ideal amounts of public goods, is all the more remarkable because it was derived under the assumption that a majority is as selfish and as devoid of scruples as a bandit. Nonetheless, it is important to recognize that the assumption that majorities and other ruling interests are self-interested is a stark simplification.

There is a far greater danger of error arising from my assumption that majorities are coherent enough to serve their interests. As we shall see later, the assumption that majorities and other ruling interests behave as though they were optimizing monoliths—though it definitely captures some crucial aspects of reality—also abstracts from the problem of special-interest groups. Though we will readily be able to deal with this problem later, it is a good reminder that, just as simplification is indispensable for intellectual progress, it is dangerous to forget what has been assumed away. Thus, the foregoing theory must be accompanied by the warning: use with caution! The question is how the theory offered here compares with alternatives.

As it happens, with one partial exception, there is nothing in the way of alternative theories that deal with the issues examined in Chapters 1 and 2. Mostly, there is only a jumble of ad hoc arguments and some fancy jargon. In fact, for lack of competition, the theory I have offered is likely to win too easily: in a competition between something and nothing, something will win, even when that something leaves much to be desired.

Yet there is one fascinating alternative prototheory emerging in the literature. This alternative is still being formulated and has not been set out in a general (and, at the same time, clear and precise) way. Some parts of the alternative theory are presented in rigorous formal models, but these models lack generality. Thus, the alternative theory or prototheory needs some additional development before its full potential will be apparent, and I will attempt to develop it in this chapter. Though I shall ultimately find that the alternative theory will not do the job that the theory in Chapters 1 and 2 does, it is useful for many purposes and will provide us with extraordinarily valuable insights. My guess is that those who enjoy economic theory will find this chapter the most interesting part of the book.

The alternative prototheory begins with an analogy to the voluntary transaction in the marketplace. Many of the best insights in the alternative theory are in the literature of what is sometimes called the Chicago School of Political Economy, but it has also benefited from advances by economists and economic historians from other intellectual traditions. To understand the alternative theory, a knowledge is required of fundamental ideas about the gains from trade, transactions costs, the theory of market failure, and Coaseian bargains. These ideas, which are generally familiar to professional economists, are explained in the next four sections: "Beginning with the Mutually Advantageous Transaction," "Transactions Costs," "Market Failures," and "The Coase Theorem."

Beginning with
the Mutually Advantageous Transaction

Generally, though many of us have bought some things that we later wished we had not purchased, we do not regret most of our transactions. The firms that sell us what we buy typically are also happy that they made the sale. Thus, everyday experience tells us that many transactions are mutually advantageous. Though those who buy from a monopolist would be better off if they could obtain a competitive price, they purchase only when they expect to gain, so even most trades with monopolists benefit both parties.

This elemental point about voluntary transactions is the single most important justification for Adam Smith's famous dictum about how self-interested parties in a market are led, as though by an invisible hand, to serve a public interest. Smith's invisible hand is at work when producers can best serve their interests by selling their output to buyers who purchase from them only when that is in the buyers' best interest. The decisions of firms about what and how much to produce are guided by their expectations about what they can profitably sell, and thus by the demands of buyers as well as by the costs of production. The production of the whole market economy is accordingly guided by firms' expectations about what trades with buyers will be mutually advantageous.

Transactions Costs

What has just been said is common to all modern economics, though it is usually not stated in a way that emphasizes the voluntary transaction as conspicuously as I have. The reason for this expositional emphasis is that it points us naturally toward another valuable idea that is fundamental to the alternative theory: the idea that it is transactions costs that limit voluntary exchange and bargaining. Just as the economists and economic historians who have been setting out the alternative theory are alert to the gains from trade and bargaining, they are also vividly aware of the transactions costs that, in their view, capture all the costs and disadvantages of the market.

In the checkout line at a supermarket, we encounter employees with the task of completing transactions. The costs of these employees and the cash registers and other facilities that they use are transactions costs: these costs and the many other kinds of transactions costs are the costs of using a market. If a market were not used, these particular costs would not be incurred. The huge literature on transactions costs in economics descends from two profound articles by the economist and Nobel laureate, Ronald Coase.[1]

Coase noted long ago that the production and activities within hierarchical firms could in principle be coordinated by the market. If hierarchical firms thrive in a competitive market, their hierarchies must be able to coordinate the production and activities that take place within the firm at a lower cost than the market would have incurred—that is, lower costs than if individual workers, suppliers of materials, and owners of machines had been spontaneously coordinated by the market. In a competitive environment, the hierarchical firms would not be viable if the goals they produced were more expensive than the market. When hierarchical firms are profitable, all the costs or disadvantages of using the market—which economists in the Coaseian tradition like to lump together and call transactions costs—must exceed the costs of using a hierarchy to coordinate that production. Economists such as Oliver Williamson have used Coase's insight to provide the best analyses we have of hierarchical firms.[2]

Market Failures

Economists consider pollution damages to be a prototypical example of market failure. If, for example, the soot coming out of a factory chimney pollutes the air for those who live near the factory, the neighborhood experiences a loss, but this loss does not show up in the costs of the firm that owns the factory. The firm presumably pays the social costs of the labor, capital, and raw materials it uses, but if it does not also pay the social costs of its pollution, then at least some of its output will tend to cost society more than it is worth (i.e., more than the price that buyers are willing to pay for its output).

The government could, by charging the firm an effluent fee determined by the social loss of the victims of the externality,[3] make the society generate more real income or welfare than before. If the situation before the effluent fee definitely was not Pareto-efficient and the effluent fee corrects this social inefficiency, it follows that there is an increase in real income or welfare, and that there must exist some distribution of this real income or welfare that will leave everyone in the society at least as well off as before and some better off. In the same way, when there is a side effect of some firms' or individuals' activity that confers a benefit on others for which there is no payment—as when firms train workers in skills that are also valuable to other firms and the workers then leave—there is too little of the activity with the valuable side effect, and an appropriate subsidy for the beneficial side effect would be needed to make the society's allocation of resources Pareto-efficient or socially rational. A. C. Pigou showed long ago that when there is an externality—when the activities of firms or individuals bring costs or benefits to others for which they are not charged or rewarded—laissez-faire cannot lead to Pareto-efficient outcomes.[4]

The feature of externalities that brings about market failure is that there is a "good" or a "bad" that does not have a price in the market because it is not feasible to charge the recipients of the "good" or to make those who generate the "bad"

pay for the losses imposed on others. Thus, any externality—
if it has an impact on two or more people—is necessarily also
a public or collective good or bad. Air pollution is a public bad
and less of it is a public good. Since less of a "bad" is always a
"good," the argument can be stated more concisely by speaking solely in terms of goods. Externality and public good problems arise because nonpurchasers cannot be kept from
consuming a good, so it cannot fetch a price in the market the
way private goods do: there is collective or group consumption and some kind of collective action or governmental action may be needed to achieve Pareto-efficiency.

When we understand that externalities that have impacts
on two or more parties are necessarily also public goods, it is
immediately evident that there are many such goods. If a
homeowner plants flowers that bring free pleasure to those
who pass by, an externality or collective good exists. The benefits of flood control, national defense, basic research, stable
price levels, inoculation against the spread of contagious diseases, and law and order generally are wholly or partly collective goods. The benefits of these goods are nonexcludable:
nonpurchasers (those who have not borne any of the costs)
cannot be excluded.

This nonexcludable character of the externality or collective good is again the source of the social inefficiency under
laissez-faire. If some individuals drive less in order to reduce
air pollution, the benefits go to those who do not curb their
driving as much as to those who do. Therefore, until the ad-
vent of the Coase theorem, all economists agreed that laissez-
faire would not deal efficiently with externalities and public
goods. Since there is little or no linkage between individual
payments or sacrifices to obtain collective goods and the enjoyment of these goods, such goods would not, in general, be

adequately provided except through compulsory tax payments or other coercive mechanisms. Since Coase's seminal article on the problem of social cost, this view has not by any means been unanimous.

The Coase Theorem

Though it has too casually come to be called a theorem, Coase's argument proceeded mainly by example. Suppose that there is a cattle ranch next to a farm and that the rancher's cattle trample the grain in the farmer's fields. On the pre-Coaseian or Pigouvian theory, this situation would have been regarded as an unambiguous example of an externality that necessarily led to market failure. The rancher does not have an incentive to take account of the losses his cattle impose on the farmer, so his way of operating and his level of operations will not be consistent with Pareto-efficiency. Efficiency would call for the rancher to be liable for the damage his cattle do to the farmer's crops.

In an argument that is one of the most famous in modern economics, Coase explained that this outcome was not necessary. If the damage costs done by the rancher's cattle to the farmer's crops exceeded the full costs of keeping them out, the cattle would tend to be kept out of the farmer's fields: voluntary bargaining between the farmer and the rancher would ensure that the externality was efficiently internalized. Moreover, so long as the rights of the parties were clearly defined, it did not matter for economic efficiency whether the law made the rancher liable for the damage his cattle did to the farmer's crops. If the rancher were not liable for the damage done by his cattle, we could still be confident that there would be a Pareto-efficient outcome: the farmer would pay the rancher to keep the cattle out of the crops. This would, of course, reduce the farmer's income, so the distribution of income between the farmer and the rancher would vary with the initial distribution of rights, but the conclusion that a Coaseian bargain would generate a socially efficient outcome was not affected by who was liable for the damage. The rancher and the farmer had an incentive to bargain until they had maximized their joint gains.

Coase was perfectly aware that bargaining could take time or could be costly for other reasons: that there were transactions costs. The externality would be internalized unless the bargaining costs were too high. But if transactions or bargaining costs were zero, all externalities would be dealt with in a Pareto-efficient way simply because rational parties would bargain until they had maximized joint gains. They would necessarily not leave any money on the table. If the outcome was not Pareto-efficient, there was still money to pick up, and so we could be certain—at least if there were no transactions or bargaining costs—that voluntary bargains among the parties at issue would generate a Pareto-efficient result. The Pigouvian theory that laissez-faire could not bring Pareto-efficiency in the presence of externalities was fundamentally wrong.

Though the issue is not usually stated this way, we can see that what Coase did, in essence, was apply the logic of mutually beneficial exchange—and the idea that transactions costs limit such trades—to the accepted theory of market failure, thereby showing that it was flawed.

Generalizing Coase

Some other economists and economic historians have tried to use the concept of voluntary exchange or Coaseian bargains—

and the transactions costs associated with them—to understand government and politics as well as the market.[5] Since the discipline of economics began with Adam Smith's account of the market and most economic analysis has focused on the market, it is natural that such an approach to government should have a special appeal to economists. When the economist's long-standing appreciation of voluntary exchange and the market is combined with an emphasis on the transactions costs or disadvantages of the market, there seems to be an opening for a general theory that might explain both economics and politics. There are many recent studies that use essentially a voluntary exchange or Coaseian bargain (from now on I shall use these terms interchangeably) and transactions costs approach to analyze government and politics. These studies sometimes differ a good deal from one another (and some of them do not even use the transactions costs label), so no brief summary could do full justice to them all. Yet it is important to consider them together, for in the aggregate they offer the best alternative theory to the one presented in Chapters 1 and 2 of this book.

The Coaseian bargain and transactions costs approach includes an awareness that transactions costs can sometimes be prohibitively high—so high that the gains from some trades would be more than offset by the expense of the needed bargaining and other transactions costs. Obviously, these transactions should not be consummated. Lost transactions use valuable resources, so it would be absurd to define economic efficiency in a way that excludes them.

Some advocates of the transactions costs approach then go on to argue that individuals and firms in society will make all of those trades that, after taking account of the transactions costs that fall upon each party, are mutually advantageous. When the transactions costs of the trade exceed the gains it would bring, the parties do not make the trade, and that too is as it should be. Thus, any status quo resulting from the market is efficient. If there had been an outcome that, after taking account of the transactions costs, was better for the participants in the economy, they would have made the deals that generated that better outcome. The phrase *market failure* is accordingly an oxymoron and laissez-faire is even better than libertarians previously thought it was. Though only a small group of anarcho-capitalist thinkers would make this matter explicit, by this logic, anarchy is also ideal. Indeed, the logic tells us that, so long as people are free to transact or not, we are automatically in the most efficient of all possible worlds!

No one should dismiss this thinking on ideological grounds, among other reasons, because it also has some very different implications. One route to these further implications is presented by the Nobel laureate economist Gary Becker and those who have built on his work. Becker has emphasized— and built a theoretical structure upon—the idea that government programs that are inefficient must be at a political disadvantage: the excess burdens that they generate mean that there are more losses—and smaller gains for winners—and these losses will be taken into account in the political bargaining. With more efficient redistributions that generate less deadweight loss there is more real income to share in political deal making. Some groups may well have more political power than others, which will affect the distribution of income, but there will be a tendency to choose economic policies that achieve the apt distribution of income with something approaching Pareto-efficiency. Thus, we observe, at least approximately, efficient redistribution.[6]

Some economists push this argument further. Transactions costs, some of them argue, depend not only on technology but also on existing institutions. The discovery of computerized point-of-sale systems, for example, has no doubt reduced some transactions costs. Similarly, the transactions costs of trading stocks in the United States have presumably been reduced by institutions such as the New York Stock Exchange and NAS-DAQ. The recognition that transactions costs depend upon institutions suddenly opens the possibility that the Coaseian case for laissez-faire or even anarchy can be stood on its head: as some point out, the government is also an institution that can reduce transactions costs. Surely most of us would agree that there are at least some types of activity or circumstances in which governments can sometimes arrange or organize transactions more efficiently than the private sector.

The Coase Theorem Holds for Politics Too!

This discovery opens the door to voluntary exchange and the transactions cost approach points to the political forces working for efficient government policies. Mutually advantageous bargaining within the political system then tends to bring about socially efficient public policies. Indeed, according to some studies, political bargaining leads to social outcomes that are Pareto-efficient, or at least approximately socially efficient. If an inefficient policy is chosen, it follows that changing to a more efficient policy must bring net gains, and that there is some distribution of these net gains that would leave everyone better off (or at least leave some better off and none worse off). Again, if there were policies that would have been able to make everyone better off, or some better off and none worse off, they would have been chosen.[7] Lo and behold, no matter how such or what kind of government interventionism is observed, the status quo is efficient.

Some of those who put forward this view previously were of an antigovernmental laissez-faire persuasion, and they have, with commendable intellectual honesty, followed the logic of their analysis of mutually advantageous transactions in the political system and arrived at a most favorable assessment of the efficiency of whatever governmental policies are chosen. Other users of the voluntary exchange and transactions cost method are much too cautious to conclude that either laissez-faire or anarchic outcomes, on the one hand, or political outcomes, on the other, are necessarily even approximately efficient. But this is a sign of their scientific caution and common sense, not of the logic of the theory: this logic inevitably has the Panglossian implications that I have described.

Why the Theory Is Utopian

It is not difficult to see how the paradigm of the mutually advantageous transaction and the transactions costs associated with it can help us account for good outcomes. When people voluntarily engage in transactions, the transactions, in the absence of fraud or mistake, make them better off. If they continue to engage in a given pattern of transactions, there must be no fraud or mistake—their interests are served. Thus, the voluntary exchange and transactions costs paradigm inevitably creates a presumption, whether we are speaking of laissez-faire or of political bargaining, that socially efficient outcomes are achieved. As we have seen, if an outcome is socially inefficient—if it does not maximize the aggregate gain of all those affected—there must exist some distribution of the gains of a more efficient outcome that would leave everyone better off. The participants in the economy can, it is argued, accordingly make the deals that achieve the gains of this more efficient outcome, unless the transactions costs exceed the gains, in which case the "more efficient" outcome is not, in fact, more efficient.

That is why, with this approach, you cannot get rid of Dr. Pangloss. If you start with the assumptions of the Coaseian bargain and transactions costs approach and make no logical mistakes, you inevitably keep coming back to the conclusion that the social equilibrium we are in or heading toward is Pareto-efficient, at least to an approximation. Whatever may be thought of the distribution of income that results from bargaining in the market and in the polity, when all the bargaining is done it tends to leave society in a situation where it is not possible to make one person better off without making someone else worse off: all the mutually advantageous deals have been made. Thus, we can see why the Coaseian bargain and transactions cost approach—even though most of the economists in this tradition are very far indeed from being utopian types—does not lend itself to explaining bad outcomes.

Patently Inefficient Social Outcomes

Yet, obviously, bad things often happen, even to rational people. Government and politics are clearly also the source of some absurdly inefficient outcomes. Partisans of the alternative theory may wonder how, in view of the foregoing logic, I can be so certain that there are absurdly inefficient outcomes. Perhaps war offers the simplest proof that there are outcomes that are not Pareto-efficient. When two countries fight a costly war, there must exist a sharing of the savings from not fighting the war that would have left both of them better off; they would, for example, be better off abiding by an agreement that had the same substantive outcome as the war and shared the savings from not fighting the war.[8]

Another manifestly bad outcome that the alternative theory cannot explain is why some countries are unnecessarily poor— earning only a tiny fraction of their potential incomes. The richest countries of the world have per-capita incomes more than twenty times as large as those of the poorest countries. All countries have access to most modern technologies and to the world's capital markets, and I have shown elsewhere that it is manifestly impossible to explain the larger part of these huge differences in per-capita income by referring to differences in the land or natural resources that they possess or to differences in the productive skills of their populations.[9]

Therefore, there is no way of explaining the extreme poverty of many nations without taking account of the extent to which they are misgoverned. Clearly, this misgovernment and the colossal differences in per-capita incomes across societies cannot plausibly be explained in terms of alleged differences in transactions costs across countries: the people in poor countries seem to be able to haggle and strike bargains just as well as those in rich countries. When the companies that make the machines embodying the most advanced technologies are anxious to sell their wares worldwide, and when there are innumerable portfolio managers who will promptly move capital to the ends of the earth for a higher risk-adjusted return, why haven't mutually advantageous transactions in modern machinery eliminated at least the most gigantic differences in per-capita incomes across countries? What transactions costs could be sufficiently high to keep a majority of the world's population in poverty when the technologies and capital that could make them more productive are readily available?

Another patently inefficient outcome, to which we shall shortly turn (mostly for other reasons), is Hobbesian anarchy. To explain anarchy and other obviously inefficient outcomes, we must recognize that not all transactions or interactions, even among totally rational parties, are voluntary.

The Dark Side of the Force

Just as individuals can often serve their interests through voluntary transactions, some of them can sometimes also serve their interests through the threat of—and sometimes the use of—force. When an individual has much more power than another, he may be better able to serve his interests by threatening to use—or by using—force than by voluntary exchange: he may be able to obtain for free what would otherwise be costly. As Thomas Schelling put it:

> One of the lamentable principles of human productivity is that it is easier to destroy than to create. A house that takes several man-years to build can be destroyed in an hour by any young delinquent who has the price of a box of matches. . . . The power to hurt—to destroy things that somebody treasures, to inflict pain and grief—is a kind of bargaining power, not easy to use but used often. In the underworld it is the basis for blackmail, extortion, and kidnapping. . . . It underlies the humane as well as the corporal punishments that society uses to deter crime and delinquency . . . and gods use it to exact obedience.[10]

Thus, the same rational self-interest that makes voluntary exchange mutually beneficial and that, when guided by the invisible hand of the market, can serve the interests of society, can lead those with power to coerce others. There is also, in Jack Hirshleifer's words, "a dark side of the force."[11]

When we drop the assumption that all interactions are voluntary, the implication that social outcomes are necessarily efficient disappears. The party with power gains from threatening to use or using that power if the cost of doing this is less than the value, to that party, of what is obtained: the losses to the victim, and even the size of these losses in relation to the gains to the party with power, do not necessarily bear on the outcome. The thief need not care whether a fence would pay him as much for what he is taking as it is worth to the victim; murderers do not kill only those who want to commit suicide.

Similarly, there is nothing that ensures that a government will necessarily confiscate the property of its subjects only when the government can use this property more efficiently than its previous owners could, or collect only those monies from taxpayers that it will spend better than they would have. Accordingly, when we pass beyond the voluntary trade and its transactions costs and include the gains from the exercise of coercive power in our analyses, there is no longer any bar to explaining the bad as well as the good things that governments do.

When we include the power to compel in the analysis, we can easily accommodate the elemental reality that governments are inherently compulsory. Taxes, for example, are by definition compulsory, and every government uses them: they are, as the proverb tells us, as inevitable as death itself. We also no longer have any problem explaining the clubs and guns that the government's police force carries, or the awesomely violent and coercive weapons of their armies, or the incredibly costly wars in which they sometimes engage. It is no accident that the symbols of governments are powerful creatures like lions and eagles rather than the cash registers or stores that we are led to expect when we consider only voluntary exchanges and transactions costs.

Coercion Is Needed for Contract Compliance

The voluntary exchange and transactions cost approach cannot, by itself, account for some good outcomes, even when these outcomes occur in socially efficient markets. Some transactions are self-enforcing. When transactions are completed on the spot, for example, the interests and the mother-wit of the parties are usually all that are needed to obtain the gains from trade. Such trades may even take place between parties without the aid of a common culture or facilitating institutions, as when autonomous tribes trade with one another, and sometimes even in the face of prohibition by government, as in black markets.

Other transactions are not self-enforcing and occur only if it is known that they will, if necessary, be enforced by a third party with coercive power. When a demander and a supplier are some distance apart, someone must be at risk for the value of the goods in transit. When goods are made to order, the inputs must be devoted to production before the transaction may be consummated. When there is insurance, some parties must make payments now in hope of indemnification if specified contingencies occur. Whenever there is a trade in futures, it is in the expectation that even a losing party will have to complete the deal. When there is lending and borrowing, capital is lent in anticipation of a return that may be due years or even decades later. In all of these cases, the gains from trade cannot be realized unless the parties expect that the contracts they make will be carried out. The borrower or whatever party whose contract fulfillment comes at a later date can always promise us that he will in time carry out his part of the deal. But, as Hobbes so famously explained, "Covenants without the sword are but words." At least as a last resort, there must be compulsory enforcement by a third party.

A theory of Coaseian bargains and the transactions costs that limit them does not explain the outside power that enforces contracts. It could easily be extended to explain why those who want to engage in transactions that require third-party enforcement want such enforcement, and why they would often be willing to pay something for it. But it cannot explain why coercive power is sometimes used to make markets work better by enforcing contracts and to take the goods that are traded in markets.

Anarchy

As we have seen, it can be rational for individuals to threaten to use coercion to serve their interests, which is, of course, the main thing that makes life in anarchies, as Thomas Hobbes put it, "solitary, poor, nasty, brutish, and short." In a Hobbesian anarchy, the incentive to produce is limited by the possibility that what one person produces—and the tools or other capital used to produce it—will be taken by others. Some of the labor in an anarchic society will be devoted to taking or stealing rather than producing.

The stealing naturally imposes costs of guarding assets and other theft-averting behavior. Since these costs are important in anarchies, and will, surprisingly, turn out to be important for understanding some nonanarchic societies, they need separate attention. Consider, for example, a family that is focusing on how it will respond to the endemic thievery in its anarchic environment. This family will best serve its interests by allocating its effort so that the last unit of effort devoted to protecting against theft has the same return as the last unit devoted to production. In an anarchy a family might rationally devote more effort to protecting against theft than to production. (Of course, the same logic applies to stealing and production, so some will devote more time to stealing than to production.)

Theft may also be averted by producing things in different ways and by producing different outputs. We have already noted that in anarchy capital goods may well be stolen, so production has to be labor intensive. Some activities, such as gathering food to eat on the spot, are inherently resistant to theft. The output forgone when less productive but theft-resistant forms of production are used is, of course, an implicit cost of anarchy.

Thus, in an anarchy the society loses the production that would have come from the resources devoted to taking, the production that would have come from the resources devoted to guarding assets, and the extra production that it would have obtained had production not been undertaken in theft-averting but socially less productive ways. Anarchy not only involves loss of life but also increases the incentives to steal and to defend against theft, and thereby reduces the incentive to produce.

Therefore, just as the powerful can sometimes rationally use violence and threats of violence to attain their ends, anarchic violence is always irrational for a society: whatever some gain by theft, others lose, and the diversion of resources to theft and theft-averting behavior reduces production. If anarchy is replaced by an appropriate peaceful order, there is a large increase in production. Indeed, the gains from switching from a violent anarchy to a peaceful order are normally so large that there are many ways to share these gains that would leave everyone in the society better off. If a population acts to serve its common interest, it will never choose anarchy.

The Social Contract: Another Name for a Coaseian Bargain

Can we conclude that, because groups gain from avoiding anarchy, they will act to avoid it? The analogy with mutually advantageous exchange suggests that they would: every anarchic society would gain from drawing up a social contract and adhering to it. The commonplace assumption that a group composed of rational people would serve whatever common or group interests it had leads to the same presumption. Can we then conclude that normally each group, because it has a common interest in avoiding anarchy, acts to serve that common interest by establishing a peaceful order?

The answer, most emphatically, is *no*. The most important reason why voluntary action to establish a peaceful order often does not occur—and never occurs for a large group or nation—is discussed in the next chapter. But we have been through one argument that is sufficient by itself to prove that many groups could not establish a social contract: even if everyone in an anarchic population signed a social contract to create a peaceful order, the anarchy would not be eliminated unless the contract was enforced. If there were a sufficiently powerful party (such as a government) that enforced contracts, there would not be anarchy in the first place.

The Indispensability of the Theory of Power

Successful as the transactions cost approach has been in the study of hierarchical firms, and suggestive as it is even in analyzing politics, it does not provide a sufficient basis for understanding government and politics, or any other sphere of life in which there is compelling authority or coercive power. It cannot explain the many patently inefficient social outcomes that we observe, nor can it, by itself, even account for those mutually advantageous contracts that require authoritative enforcement. When the idea of transactions cost is used in conjunction with an appreciation of the salience of coercive power, it can provide useful insights into politics and government (as in the work of Avinash Dixit,[12] for example). When it is used to examine two-person interactions in the presence of pollutants or other externalities, it is again extremely useful. It also proves to be suggestive when used in conjunction with the theory offered in Chapters 1 and 2 of this book. But the metaphor of voluntary and mutually advantageous bargains and the transactions costs that limit them is not enough by itself and is not even the natural starting point for a theory of government and politics.

To understand governments and all the good and bad things they do—and the horrible anarchies that emerge in their absence—there can be no substitute for a theory of power of the kind we began to develop in Chapters 1 and 2. We must understand not only the gains from voluntary exchange but also the logic of coercion and force.

Adding to the Theory

It is time to return to expanding the theory set out earlier in this book. Though we shall see in the next chapter that there is also a logical flaw in the Coaseian argument that, if transactions costs were zero, rational parties would necessarily arrive at Pareto-efficient Coaseian bargains, we go into this area only because it is necessary to understand additional theory. We must see why small groups such as hunter-gatherer bands normally work out what are, in effect, social contracts that provide a peaceful order and other public goods within the band, and why no substantial population has ever worked out a voluntary Coaseian bargain. We also need to understand the main force that is undermining the economic vitality of even the most prosperous economies in the world.

4

RATIONAL INDIVIDUALS
AND IRRATIONAL SOCIETIES

S UPPOSE A GROUP OF INDIVIDUALS suffers from an outcome that is not efficient or rational for that group—that
is, one that does not maximize the aggregate or joint real income or welfare of the individuals in the group. As the alternative theory in Chapter 3 reminds us, it would seem to
follow that there must be a deal (a Coaseian bargain) that
would share the gains from changing to an efficient or group-
optimal outcome in such a way that each and every individual
in the group would be better off.

Ronald Coase's conclusion that, if transactions costs were
zero, this group-rational outcome would be achieved, is almost universally accepted. This proposition is believed to
hold everywhere and for all kinds and all sizes of groups. To be
sure, everyone knows that it could be that the bargaining or
transactions costs of making a group-efficient deal could be
greater than the gains from the change to the "efficient" allocation. We know that this would mean (if the best mechanisms for transactions, whether formal or informal, private or
governmental, were used) that the alternative allocation was
not truly efficient in the first place. Thus, the Coaseian logic,
at least as it has been extended by some transactions cost

economists, appears to imply that groups, if they are made up of rational individuals, are also rational: that groups will tend to act in their common interests much as individuals tend to act in their individual interests.

This belief is by no means peculiar to the transactions costs or Chicagoan traditions, and for a long time it was (and, in some circles, still is) the conventional wisdom. Marx's theory of class, for example, makes the assumption that a social class made up of rational and informed individuals (one without false consciousness) will act in its class interest. Capitalist societies are controlled by the bourgeois class and, at an appropriate stage of capitalist development, the proletariat will act in its interest to overthrow capitalism, establish a dictatorship of the proletariat, and create the basis for a classless and stateless communist society. The group theory or analytical pluralism that once dominated political science attempted to explain politics on the premise that groups tended to act in their group interest, and some economists' theories of labor unions made the same assumption about groups of workers. The idea that people, because of the evils of anarchy and the gains from a peaceful order, establish a social contract to create a government is yet another example of the assumption that groups tend to act in their interests much as individuals do.

I have shown in a book on *The Logic of Collective Action*[1] that the view that groups tend to act in their interests is wrong. The argument in that book is now, for most contexts, almost universally accepted. Yet there are also a few important contexts—the Coase theorem is one—where the argument is not applied, apparently because it is assumed to have no pertinence (or is never even considered). Luckily, the Coaseian logic considered in the Chapter 3 suggests some new extensions of the logic of collective action and also a new way of demonstrating that logic. It also turns out that the new demonstration reveals some common and most harmful misinterpretations of the famous Prisoner's Dilemma model, especially with respect to the relationship between the number of individuals in a group and the likelihood the group will act to serve its common interests.

When we have a correct understanding of both the Coase theorem and the Prisoner's Dilemma, we will have added considerable explanatory power to the theory offered in this book. In this chapter I offer a somewhat different explanation of the logic of collective action than before. Though it is true that those who already have a good understanding of *The Logic of Collective Action* will find it sufficient to understand the remaining chapters of this book, they will also find some surprises in the present chapter. I begin with a familiar point about the ability of small groups to act collectively.

Small Groups Often Succeed in Voluntary Collective Action

In groups with only a few members, one party by itself often obtains sufficient benefit from a collective good that it gains from providing some of the good entirely at its own expense. The other parties then obtain a free ride. For an extreme case, consider a public good that benefits only two parties, such as a cul-de-sac road that serves just a pair of households, and suppose also that the two households place an equal value on the collective good. It is easily possible that a minimal supply of a public good would, when the gains to both parties are added together, be worth more than twice what it costs. Then each household would gain from providing some amount of the collective good, even if it bore all of the cost. Each household would obtain half of the benefit of any action it took in the interest of the group of two.

Now suppose that there were, say, five households that would benefit from the cul-de-sac road. The average household would then receive a fifth of the benefit that resulted from a contribution it made to the provision of the collective good. This incentive would often motivate contributions to the provision of a collective good, though obviously there is not as strong an incentive for group-oriented action as in the group of two. An average household in the group of five could not gain from providing any of the good entirely at its own expense unless the aggregate benefits of some amount of the collective good to all members were five or more times as great as the total cost of this quantity. Minimal amounts of many goods can be so valuable in relation to their cost that this condition is sometimes met. Thus, it is possible that there might be some unilateral provision even for a group of five, though it would be much less in relation to the need or common interest or rational-for-the-group amount than for the group of two. Usually a larger number of households would need a longer or stronger road, but even if this were not the case, it is still certain that unilateral behavior would provide less of the collective good in relation to the collectively rational or group-optimal level of provision.

Strategic Interaction

When the number who would benefit from the provision of a collective good is small, there is also an incentive for each party to interact strategically and to bargain. For example, one party may say to another, "I will provide some amount (or pay a share of the cost of any units provided) if you also do so." When a potential beneficiary of a collective good knows that another will match its provision or share the costs of provision, that reduces the cost of each unit of the public good to each party and increases the likelihood that some amount of the good will be provided. When a pair who have arrived at an agreement to share costs say that they will both share if another does, a third party will find that the value of a contribution is increased even more. Cost sharing not only makes provision of some amount of a collective good more likely but also leads to provision of a larger quantity. If the costs of providing a collective good are shared by all those who value it in exact proportion to the benefit they receive from it, each will want an amount that maximizes the aggregate gain: that is, there will be a group-rational (group optimal or Pareto-efficient for the group) level of provision.

Normally, when the number of potential beneficiaries of a collective good is small, the interests of each are significantly affected by the contributions or noncontributions of the others. Imagine that the members of a group are providing a group-optimal amount and consider what happens if a member stops contributing. In a group of five households that place an equal value on the collective good, if one backs out of a matching or cost-sharing scheme, the costs to the remainder go up substantially. The increase in dues is noticeable, so each of the remaining four takes note of the free riding. When each contributor must bear a fourth rather than a fifth of the cost of a marginal unit, each wants to purchase a noticeably smaller quantity. In turn, the free rider also enjoys noticeably less of the collective good than before, which may make the free rider start paying dues again.

If it does not, the other members can increase the incentive to the free rider to contribute again by cutting back to a lower provision or no provision. In sufficiently small groups, we can always be sure that there is an incentive to continue bargaining until mutually advantageous collective action has taken place. This is because each party's contribution makes a significant difference to each of the others, so they have an incentive to bargain with one another. Though there is no certainty that small groups will provide themselves with a collective good, voluntary behavior and bargaining will often succeed. Except for a very special case to which we turn next, an outcome without provision cannot be a stable equilibrium: since there is a continuing incentive for each party to bargain with the others, and to carry on bargaining until gains from collective action are achieved, an outcome without provision is not an equilibrium.

The Commonplace Error

There is still a commonplace assumption that even groups of only two parties will not cooperate in their common interest. Even some technically sophisticated researchers take it for granted that groups composed of only two members are as likely to fail to serve their common interests as are large groups. This common misconception is apparently due to the enchanting simplicity of one famous example.

The beguilingly simple example is that of the famous Prisoner's Dilemma. A prevalent conclusion drawn from the Prisoner's Dilemma example is that even groups of only two members normally fail to obtain a collective good. It is only when two individuals repeat the Prisoner's Dilemma game an indefinitely large number of times that they are likely to achieve the gains from cooperation. In any single game (or in any set of games where the players know in advance how many games will be played), the dominant strategy for each player is to defect rather than to cooperate, so a collectively rational outcome is not obtained.

In the Prisoner's Dilemma metaphor, two prisoners are already in the hands of the police and can be proven guilty of a lesser offense than the one with which the analysis is concerned. The two criminals have committed the more serious offense, but they were the only ones who observed this crime and neither can be convicted unless at least one of them confesses and implicates the other. Thus, keeping silent about the crime they have jointly committed is a collective good to the two criminals.

One key to why criminals are used to illustrate the failure of social cooperation is that the prisoners can be, and are in the canonical metaphor, isolated in separate cells by the police. The prisoners are thereby denied communication with each other. Because the two prisoners are not allowed to communicate, they have no opportunity to make an agreement not to tell the authorities about their participation in the crime at issue, and therefore no opportunity to serve their collective interest by making it impossible for the state to convict either of them of the more serious offense. A driving force in the two-person Prisoner's Dilemma is that an almost universal feature of any interaction of two individuals with a common problem—communication about how to obtain the outcome that is a collective good for both of them—is prevented by some exceptionally special circumstances: police officers who know that communication between the prisoners can stand in the way of inducing them to squeal on each other.

If it is to serve their common interest in avoiding conviction for the more serious offense, an agreement between the two prisoners that neither will testify to the crime they have

committed must be credible. Note the second special circumstance of this dilemma: the prisoners, because an agreement
to obstruct justice is itself illegal, are unable to make a contract enforceable through the courts. Therefore, it is no accident that, of all people, it is criminals who are used to show
the difficulties of social cooperation in groups with as few as
two members. In fact, when a small number of individuals
would benefit from a collective good, they can normally communicate with one another about how to cooperate in their
common interest, and they usually have access to legal agreements as well as other mechanisms to enforce their deals.
They can therefore usually obtain a collective good and
thereby serve their collective interest.

The logic in this chapter, showing that sufficiently small
groups can often engage in collective action, applies in all those
cases where the parties involved are able to communicate with
one another and are able to make enforceable agreements. (In
collective action, as in trade in private goods, agreements are
normally self-enforcing when the contributions of the parties
are essentially simultaneous [that is, like an on-the-spot mar-
ket], and normally require third-party enforcement when the
contributors make contributions at different times.)

Since small groups typically can communicate and take advantage of available devices to enforce agreements, we must
ask why an example that is true only in exceptional circumstances became so famous and influential. Probably part of
the reason is that it is such a beautifully simple example. But
another reason is that the conclusion of the Prisoner's
Dilemma—that groups will not cooperate to achieve their collective interests—is true for large groups, though it does not
capture the real reasons why large groups do not succeed in
voluntarily achieving their collective interests.

Why Voluntary Collective Action
Must Fail in Large Groups

Suppose that there are, say, a million potential beneficiaries of a collective good. It was obvious in our earlier analysis of small groups that an average individual in a group of, say, five, would receive a fifth of the benefit of an action in the interest of the group. A representative person in a group of a million potential beneficiaries of a collective good will obtain only a millionth of the benefit of the contribution he or she makes to the provision of the collective good. The person in a group of a million is in a position similar to that of the individual criminal in a populous society. In a really large group, the typical individual receives only a minuscule share of the benefit of an action he or she takes in the group interest. This minuscule share does not typically motivate individuals in a large group to voluntarily act in a way that is consistent with the common interest of the group.

It might seem that a collective good could conceivably have such a fantastically high benefit-cost ratio that even one-millionth of the benefit would exceed the total cost of one unit, or some units, of the good, so some would be provided unilaterally. But if the benefit–cost ratio were that high, there would be a truly colossal collective irrationality! At the group optimum, a marginal dollar of expenditure on the collective good would, of course, have a benefit-cost ratio of one. If the value of a collective good should be so great in relation to its cost that a typical individual in a large group had an incentive to provide some, that would prove that the group was failing in a big way to serve its collective interests.

Moreover, individuals who obtain only a millionth of the benefit from provision of a collective good typically do not have an incentive to interact strategically or to bargain. If each individual obtains only one-millionth of the benefit from a provision of the collective good, two people would receive only two-millionths of the benefit, and two-millionths of the benefit is normally not enough to motivate a pair of individuals to bargain with a third individual to remedy the collectively irrational outcome for the group.

The Perverse Logic of Threats of Nonprovision

Even if many individuals in a large group worked out an arrangement to provide some of the collective good, these individuals would not gain as much as free riders in the group. It is true that the individuals who by agreement provided some amount of the collective good could threaten each free rider that they would cease providing unless the free rider contributed. But such bargaining threats are not likely to work. Think of a group of N individuals who would benefit from receiving a public good. Any subset of $N - 1$ who are not free riding could threaten to provide nothing unless a holdout pays an appropriate share.

Although we have seen that this strategy can often work in smaller groups, as a group gets larger this threat becomes less and less credible; in a group of a thousand, an average beneficiary of the collective good who uses a holdout strategy knows that the other 999 would in the aggregate lose 999 times as much from nonprovision as he or she does. Moreover, an average rational beneficiary in a group of a thousand could not possibly be induced by nonprovision to pay very much more than one-thousandth of the total cost of the collective good. Thus, the gain to the 999 from the bargaining strategy of nonprovision, even if it is successful, is bound to be small in relation to their loss from nonprovision.

In short, in any really large group, the only threat that is available in the absence of coercion—the threat of nonprovision—is virtually certain to fail for two reasons. First, a large group of providers loses many times more from nonprovision than each target of their bargaining tactic. Second, they also lose much more than they could obtain, over the same length of time, from a free rider in contributions.

Everyone has an incentive to try to be in a free-rider or hold-out position. It follows that we should not expect that the majority will, in fact, be contributing to the provision of a collective good. The outcome of voluntary interaction in sufficiently large groups that would profit from obtaining a collective good is often no provision whatsoever, and never the voluntary, unsubsidized provision of anything remotely resembling a collectively rational level.

The Logic at the Margin of Group Rationality

Since voluntary individual behavior in large groups cannot obtain collectively rational quantities of collective goods, if it obtains any at all, we must make an imaginative effort to think of a situation where a group-optimal amount has already been provided. Yet we have done that with the small group and it is interesting to consider the contrast. If a group of a million was obtaining a group-optimal quantity of a collective good, then the aggregate benefit to the million beneficiaries from the last unit provided would just equal the cost of this marginal unit. But then the average individual in this group of a million would obtain one-millionth of the benefit of this marginal unit. So the average member would find that, if he provided a unit of the collective good, it would be worth to him only one-millionth of its cost! Clearly, large groups will not obtain collectively rational amounts of collective goods through voluntary and unsubsidized individual behavior.

Since *The Logic of Collective Action* was published in 1965, researchers in several disciplines and diverse countries have undertaken a vast number of detailed studies, statistical tests, and even controlled experiments to test the foregoing theory. An overwhelming majority of research has corroborated it. Some of the literature growing out of *The Logic of Collective Action* is cited, if not summarized, in two books, which also add important contributions of their own: Russell Hardin's *Collective Action*[2] and Todd Sandler's book of the same title.[3]

Even When There Are No Transactions Costs . . .

Some students of transactions costs suppose that, since everyone in a large group could be made better off if all agreed to pay their share of the costs and the collective good was provided, even groups of thousands or millions could voluntarily provide themselves with collective goods if some outside source paid for the costs of the needed bargaining or if for any reason there were no transactions or bargaining costs. After all, an agreement to share costs in proportion to benefits and to provide the good would be a unanimously advantageous agreement, so the Coaseian bargaining and transactions cost approach leads us to think that it would happen if the parties to the agreement did not have to pay the costs of the bargaining.

The assumption that some outside source pays all transactions costs is of course unrealistic, and we have seen that the individuals in a sufficiently large group would not, in the absence of an outside bargaining cost subsidy, even have an incentive to bargain with one another. Yet it is important to think about what would happen if transactions or bargaining costs were paid by an outside source or were zero for other reasons, since it illuminates a crucial and heretofore unnoticed difference between transactions involving private goods and those involving public goods. The failure to notice this difference has led many economists into logical error. Therefore, let us assume that some outside foundation pays the full costs of time and other resources that the individuals in a large group would devote to negotiating a unanimously advantageous voluntary agreement to provide themselves with a collective good.

With transactions in private goods, the only way to obtain such goods is to be part of the transaction; if you are cut out of the deal, you obtain nothing. There is no problem in obtaining the participation of the relevant parties to a mutually advantageous transaction in private goods: the interests of the parties in obtaining the benefits motivate their participation.

The costs of learning about an opportunity for a mutually advantageous transaction—or other transactions costs—may keep some deals from being made that would otherwise have been mutually advantageous, but obtaining information and covering other transactions costs uses up valuable resources, so we should not assume there is any social inefficiency when such deals are not made. The self-interest of individuals gives them an incentive to search for advantageous transactions and often it will pay firms to sell information about such market opportunities and to engage in brokerage. Accordingly, even though markets are characteristically imperfect in diverse ways, there is no general problem for societies in motivating individuals and firms to participate in mutually advantageous transactions in private goods.

A Game Without a Core

Now suppose that there is a large group in which everyone would be better off if the costs of a collective good were shared by all and the good provided. Suppose further that most of the potential beneficiaries of the collective good—or all but one of them—have agreed to share costs and provide the collective good. Those who are not part of the deal are the luckiest of all: they obtain the public good for nothing, whereas those who are part of the deal pay the costs! The best possible outcome is to be cut out of the deal.

Potential beneficiaries are not, in fact, cut out of deals, because it is in the interest of those who make a deal to have everyone else sharing the costs. Instead, if it appears there will be a deal to provide a collective good, rational individuals go out of their way to cut themselves out. Since, in general, each person would be best off if there were a deal to provide a collective good that he or she were not part of, there is an incentive for everyone to be in just that position, and this works against a deal to provide a collective good from the beginning.[4]

To see the importance of this, think not only of the whole group but also of all of the possible coalitions or subgroups (including subgroups of a single individual) of which an individual in the group of potential beneficiaries could try to be a part. Suppose as well that the collective good at issue comes in only one discrete quantity, so we can abstract from the question of how much is provided and think only about whether any of the good will be provided. The problem of collective action arises— and the possibility of a Coaseian bargain becomes an issue—

only if the public good is worth more to the whole group than it costs, so we assume that this is true by a large margin.

It follows that there has to be some division of the costs of providing the collective good such that each and every member of the whole group would be better off if it were provided than if it were not. One division of the costs that would certainly qualify would be for each member of the whole group to pay a share of the costs equal to that individual's share of the benefits (a Lindahl share); if all of the members of the group were identical, they would all pay an equal share of the cost of the public good. Let us suppose that this is the division of costs that is at issue.

Thus, we definitely have a situation where, when there are no transactions costs, the Coase theorem tells us that rational individuals would make a Coaseian bargain to provide the public good. With the fair share allocation of the costs, every individual in the group would gain from provision of the collective good.

But would there be any smaller coalitions or subgroups that would offer a prospect of a larger payoff for an individual? Definitely—and for large group collective action problems, necessarily—the answer is *yes*. The coalition or subgroup that free rides will obviously gain the most when others pay for the good! This is true whether there are many free riders or only one. A goal of rational individuals in the group as a whole is to free ride while others pay. If the public good is not provided, that contradicts the Coase theorem in these cases where there are assumed to be no transactions or bargaining costs.

If individuals in the larger group believe that the collective good will be provided, they will try to maneuver themselves into the group that does not pay and maneuver others into the coalition that shares the costs: that is the rational strategy. If transactions costs are covered by an outside source or are zero for another reason—so the strategic maneuvering costs nothing—the maneuvering will go on indefinitely with no assurance that the collective good will be provided! Whether individuals believe the public good will be provided or not, the prediction of the Coase theorem that, with zero transactions costs, rational individuals will always make a Coaseian bargain, is disproved.[5]

The general point is that large group collective action problems always involve what the cooperative game theorists call *games without cores:*[6] situations where some individuals are better off in a subgroup than in a coalition of the whole, even when total gains are greatest from a coalition of the whole.[7] It is sometimes supposed that the assumption that there are no transactions costs by definition does away with everything that could possibly prevent rational individuals from achieving Coaseian bargains. But the difficulty that has just been delineated cannot be assumed or defined away, for it involves a logical contradiction: the Coase theorem assumes rational individual behavior and makes no sense without it, but in large group collective action problems, rational individual behavior implies that individuals will try to cut themselves out of Coaseian bargains and thereby often prevent the Coaseian bargains from occurring, even when transactions costs are zero.

Selective Incentives

Large groups can engage in collective action when they have access to a selective incentive, which, unlike the collective good itself, applies selectively to individuals depending on whether they contribute to the provision of the collective good. A selective incentive can be either negative or positive;

it can, for example, be a loss or punishment imposed only on those who do not help provide the collective good. Tax payments are, of course, obtained with the help of negative selective incentives, since those who do not pay their taxes are then liable for both taxes and penalties.

The best-known type of organized interest group in modern democratic societies, the labor union, is also usually supported, in part, through negative selective incentives. Most of the dues in those unions with real power are obtained through union shop, closed shop, or agency shop arrangements that make dues paying more or less compulsory and automatic. There are often informal arrangements with the same effect. Picketing during strikes is another negative selective incentive that unions sometimes need. Although picketing in industries with established and stable unions is usually peaceful, this is because the union's capacity to close down an enterprise against which it has called a strike is clear to all; the early phase of unionization often involves a great deal of violence on the part of both unions and antiunion employers and strike-breaking workers.

Some opponents of labor unions argue that, since many of the members of labor unions join only through legally enforced union shop arrangements, most of the relevant workers do not want to be unionized. The Taft-Hartley Act, passed in the United States shortly after World War II, provided that impartial governmentally administered elections should be held to determine whether workers did in fact want to belong to unions. As the collective-good logic set out here suggests, the same workers who had to be coerced to pay union dues voted for the unions with compulsory dues (and normally by overwhelming margins), so this feature of the Taft-Hartley Act was soon abandoned as pointless. The workers who avoided paying union dues but voted to force everyone to pay dues are no different from taxpayers who vote, in effect, for high levels of taxation, yet try to arrange their private affairs to avoid taxes.

Because of the same logic, many professional associations also get members through covert or overt coercion (for example, lawyers in U.S. states with a "closed bar"). So do lobbies and cartels of several other types; some of the contributions by corporate officials, for instance, to politicians useful to the corporation are also the result of subtle forms of coercion.

Positive selective incentives, although easily overlooked, are also commonplace, as diverse examples in *The Logic of Collective Action* demonstrate. American farm organizations offer prototypical examples. Many members of the stronger American farm organizations are members because their dues payments are automatically deducted from the patronage dividends of farm cooperatives or are included in the insurance premiums paid to mutual insurance companies associated with the farm organizations. Any number of organizations with urban clients also provide similar positive selective incentives in the form of insurance policies, publications, discounted prices, and other private goods made available only to members. The grievance procedures of labor unions usually also offer selective incentives, since the grievances of active members often get the most attention.

The symbiosis between the political power of a lobbying organization and the business institutions associated with it often yields tax or other advantages for the business institution, and the publicity and other information flowing out of the political arm of a movement often generates patterns of preference or trust that make the business activities of the movement more remunerative. The surpluses obtained in such ways in turn provide positive selective incentives that recruit participants for the lobbying efforts, so the business and lobbying activities are complementary, which means they can be viable even in the most competitive environments.

A Recapitulation

The longstanding belief that groups normally act in their common interests—notwithstanding its reinforcement from the Coase theorem, Marx, and diverse other intellectual traditions—is wrong. Whenever the value of a collective good to any group unambiguously exceeds its costs, there necessarily is a potential Coaseian bargain to provide the good that (if made and enforced) would leave everyone in the group better off. But, if a group is sufficiently large, its members will not have any incentive to engage in the costly bargaining and strategic interaction that would work out such a Coaseian bargain. Even if transactions costs were zero, there is no presumption that they would work out a Coaseian bargain: any expectation that a Coaseian bargain would be made would generate a game without a core—a continuing effort of all rational individuals to be in the subgroup that obtained the largest gains, the coalition of free riders.

Groups can overcome the great difficulties of collective action and rationally serve their collective interests only in two circumstances. One is when the numbers in the group are few: notwithstanding the opposite conclusion suggested by commonplace misinterpretations of the Prisoner's Dilemma, sufficiently small groups can and very often do act in their common interests. The other circumstance that can enable a group to overcome the difficulties of collective action is the availability of selective incentives. Since many groups are large and have no opportunity to obtain selective incentives, they can never act in their collective interests.

No society can ever have a comprehensive and symmetrical organization of all groups. Accordingly, such groups as the unemployed, the poor, the consumers, and the taxpayers are not organized. Thus, a bargain among groups organized for collective action will tend to ignore the losses to the unorganized: voluntary or market forces cannot lead to a Coaseian bargain or social contract that is efficient for the society as a whole. As we shall see later, it also takes a long time for groups that can conquer the difficulties of collective action to overcome them.

5

GOVERNANCE AND ECONOMIC GROWTH

I F THE ARGUMENT THAT HAS BEEN DEVELOPED in the previous chapters is right, we now have the tools we need to answer many important questions. These include the issue raised in Chapter 3 about why some groups overcome anarchy by voluntary agreement and some do not. They also include some of the questions posed in the Preface about why the results (especially in relation to expectations) were so different after the defeat of fascism and the collapse of communism. Why were there unexpected economic miracles after the defeat of fascism, whereas economic performance was often even worse after the collapse of communism than it had been while it prevailed?

The Evolution of Governance

I shall first provide the answer promised in Chapter 3 about why large populations cannot eliminate anarchy and establish government through a voluntary social contract or Coaseian bargain, whereas many smaller groups can achieve a peaceful order by voluntary agreement. We noted that the gains from eliminating anarchy are so great that everyone can become better off, and that a peaceful order is a public good. To understand the provision of a peaceful order and other collective goods, we examined the logic of collective action, revealing that the difficulties of voluntary collective action increase dramatically as the number who benefit from a collective good increases. Thus, small groups, though it might take them time to work out the agreements necessary to obtain collectively rational levels of provision, typically will be able to engage in voluntary collective action, but large groups cannot serve their common interests through voluntary (and unsubsidized) behavior. The theory accordingly predicts that large populations will not be able to obtain a peaceful order through the voluntary social contracts that political philosophers often discuss or through any other kind of voluntary collective action, but that small groups often will obtain a peaceful order by consensus.

These theoretical expectations are very much in keeping with the historical record and the anthropological literature. In spite of the vast literature on social contracts—and the gains a society would have if such contracts were made and implemented—no one has ever found a large society that obtained a peaceful order or other public goods through a Coaseian bargain among the individuals in the society. There is no case in the historical record that I can find where any substantial population has, through voluntary collective action of any kind, established a peaceful order.

By contrast, the anthropological literature suggests that the most primitive communities, through voluntary action, achieve a peaceful order. The simplest food-gathering and hunting societies are normally made up of bands that have, including the children, only about fifty or a hundred people.

Such a band normally contains only a few families that need to cooperate, so they are small groups. As the theory predicts, they are normally voluntary groups and are typically governed by consensus. Many of the most primitive tribes are acephalous, so there often is not an individual in a position to coerce the others. When such bands have a chief, the chief often only presides over and implements collective decisions. When a band becomes too large or disagreement is intense, the band may split, but the new bands normally also make decisions by unanimous consent. If a tribe is in the hunting and gathering stage, there is little or no incentive for anyone to subjugate another tribe or to keep slaves, since captives cannot generate enough surplus above subsistence to justify the costs of guarding them.[1] The anthropologists' finding that primitive tribes normally maintain peace and order by voluntary agreement is also broadly in keeping with what Tacitus and Caesar and other classical writers observed among the less advanced Germanic tribes.

It is now natural to ask what happens when populations grow and become too large to obtain a peaceful order through voluntary collective action. Once tribal peoples learned how to raise crops effectively, production increased and populations grew. There were eventually large populations that needed governments. If voluntary collective action cannot obtain the gains from a peaceful order or other public goods, how did these larger populations obtain a peaceful order? As we saw in Chapter 1, autocrats can pay themselves very well indeed. So it pays any roving bandit leader—or anyone else who is strong enough—to become a stationary bandit, which is why most large populations over the course of human history have been governed by autocrats.[2] The analysis in Chapter 2 also explained how, albeit only in lucky circumstances, representative government or democracy could emerge autonomously. Thus, the logic that has been offered covers the major types of governments and is broadly consistent with their evolution over time.

Sclerosis in Societies with Freedom of Organization

I conceded earlier that the assumption in Chapter 1 that majorities (and other ruling interests that earned income in the market) were coherent and purposive was much too simple. It was possible, by modeling majorities as though they were optimizing monoliths, to illuminate some important features of reality. The encompassing and sometimes even superencompassing interests of majorities are very important in explaining why many democracies have done as well as they have. Alas, the analysis of the encompassing and superencompassing interest of majorities, taken by itself, leaves us with a much too rosy view.

It is too rosy in part because the typical citizen has no incentive to engage in serious study of public affairs or of what effects different types of public policies and institutions will really have. Consider a typical citizen who is deciding how much time to devote to studying the policies or leadership of his or her country. The more time the citizen devotes to this matter, the greater the likelihood that a vote will be cast in favor of rational policies and good leadership. This typical citizen will, however, get only a small share of the gain from the more effective policies and leadership: in the aggregate, the other residents of the country will get almost all the gains, so the individual citizen does not have an incentive to devote much time to fact finding and to thinking about what would be best for the country. Knowledge about the public's business is a public good, and the same collective action logic applies to the study of the public's business as applies to other public goods.

The "Rational Ignorance" of the Typical Citizen

The typical voter is, accordingly, "rationally ignorant" about what choices would best serve the interest of the electorate or any majority in it. This point is most dramatically evident in national elections. The gain to a voter from studying issues and candidates until it is clear what vote is truly in his or her interest is given by the difference between the value to the individual only (rather than the society) of the "right" and the "wrong" election outcomes, multiplied by the probability that a change in the individual's vote will alter the outcome of the election. Since the probability that a typical voter will change the outcome of the election is vanishingly small, the typical citizen, whether he or she is a physician or a taxi driver, is usually rationally ignorant about public affairs.

Sometimes information about public affairs is so interesting or entertaining that acquiring it for these reasons alone pays; this situation appears to be the single most important source of exceptions to the generalization that typical citizens are rationally ignorant about public affairs. Similarly, individuals in a few special vocations can receive considerable rewards in private goods if they acquire exceptional knowledge of public goods. Politicians, lobbyists, journalists, and social scientists, for example, may earn more money, power, or prestige from knowledge of public affairs. Occasionally, exceptional knowledge of public policy can generate exceptional profits in stock exchanges or other markets. Withal, the typical citizen will usually find that his or her income and life chances will not be improved by the zealous study of public affairs or even of any single collective good.

The fact that the benefits of individual enlightenment about public goods are usually dispersed throughout a group or nation, rather than concentrated upon the individual who bears the costs of becoming enlightened, explains many phenomena. It explains, for example, the "man bites dog" criterion of what is newsworthy. If the television newscasts were watched or newspapers were read solely to obtain the most important information about public affairs, aberrant events of little public importance would be ignored and the complexities of economic policy and quantitative analyses of public problems would be emphasized. When the news is, by contrast, largely an alternative to other forms of diversion or entertainment for most people, intriguing oddities and human-interest items are in demand. Similarly, events that unfold in a suspenseful way or sex scandals among public figures are fully covered by the media. Public officials, often able to thrive without giving the citizens good value for their taxes, may fall over an exceptional mistake that is simple and striking enough to be newsworthy. Protests and demonstrations that may offend a significant portion of the public make diverting news and therefore call attention to arguments that might otherwise be ignored.

The rational ignorance of electorates—and thus of majorities—means that majorities will often fail to see their true interests. They can be the victims of predations that they do not notice. They can be persuaded by superficially plausible arguments that a given policy is in the interest of the majority or of the society as a whole, when it really only serves some special interest. When we consider the incentives facing special-interest groups, we see that this problem is very serious.

The Organization of Individual Industries and Occupations

Consider situations where the firms or workers in an industry or the individuals employed in some occupation or profession are organized to act collectively, as a lobby or a cartel. They are not a majority of the electorate and are unlikely to earn a substantial percentage of the national income of a country. Because they are not a majority, they cannot obtain complete control of the taxation and spending power of a government. They must instead take advantage of the rational ignorance of the electorate about the specifics of public policy and about the actual effects of public policies.

Thus, they persuade rationally ignorant electorates that protection for their industry strengthens the national economy or that regulations that limit entry and competition in their industry are good for the consumer, or they obtain tax loopholes and subsidies that the average voter does not know about. They often will be able to unobtrusively collude or cartelize their markets and thus obtain monopoly prices or wages. The fact that special-interest groups best serve their interests by pushing for measures that are easily misunderstood or unlikely to be widely noticed normally makes the loss in economic efficiency from their activities greater than it would be if they received straightforward and unconditional subsidies.

To what extent will the organizations for collective action that represent particular industries or occupations have an incentive to refrain from redistribution to themselves that would do great damage to economic efficiency? The profits and even the value added in a typical industry and the wages in a typical craft or occupation are a small fraction of gross domestic product (GDP). Suppose, for ease of calculation, that a

given organized interest obtains exactly 1 percent of the GDP.
Then it will pay this organized interest to press for both governmental and cartelistic redistributions to itself up to the
point where the social losses are 100 times as great as the
amount it obtains! Only then will its marginal share of these
social losses be as great as its gain at the margin from further
redistribution. Thus, the typical special-interest group has a
very narrow rather than an encompassing interest. It faces incentives that are by no means as wholesome as those facing
majorities. Unfortunately, they are much more detrimental to
society than those facing the secure stationary bandit, often
also worse than those that face the gang with a protection
racket, and not much better for society than those facing the
individual criminal. Since I have discussed this issue carefully
in a book on *The Rise and Decline of Nations*,[3] I will not go
into this matter any further here.

The Slow Emergence of Organization
for Collective Action

Chapter 4 argued that collective action is difficult and prob-
lematic. In addition, there are normally some special start-up
costs in creating an organization or new pattern of cooperation. Even small groups or groups with a selective incentive
that could in principle be worked out may not be able to organize until favorable circumstances emerge. Each party wants
to bear the lowest possible share of the costs and in bargaining
has an incentive to hold out, sometimes for an indefinitely
long time. Some of the collective action that is attainable
through bargaining in small groups will not be attained until
some time has passed.

In larger groups, where collective action is attainable only through selective incentives, even greater difficulties must be overcome. If coercion is the selective incentive, the coercive force has to be arranged, and since people do not like to be co-erced, there is difficulty and even danger. Strong leadership and favorable circumstances are usually required. The beginning of the union career of Jimmy Hoffa illustrates this point. The young Hoffa was one of the workers in an unorganized warehouse in Detroit. On a hot summer day, a large shipment of strawberries that would soon spoil arrived, and Hoffa then persuaded his co-workers to strike. The employer found it better to accept Hoffa's demands than to lose his perishable cargo. Usually the circumstances are not so favorable, and leaders with the cunning, courage, and lack of inhibition that characterized Jimmy Hoffa are not on the scene.

Positive selective incentives can be found, if at all, only after a great deal of effort. Generating a surplus that can finance provision of a collective good or induce others to provide it is inherently chancy—there are failures as well as successes among those who attempt to create new businesses. And entrepreneurs who make money naturally often keep it for themselves. Thus, usually some complementarity between the activity that can provide a collective good and that which produces income must be found or exploited; lobbying power must be used in part to get favorable governmental treatment of the business activity, for example, or the reputation and trust of the lobbying organization among its beneficiaries must be exploited by the associated business activity. Even when such complementarities can be exploited, they may be discovered or worked out only after some time, and then only if there are imaginative leaders.

Testing the Argument

I have argued that it takes a long time for a society to accumulate many organizations for collective action, and that industry-specific, occupation-specific, and other narrow organizations for collective action are most harmful to economic efficiency and dynamism. Because majorities have encompassing and sometimes even superencompassing interests, democratic governments that are not influenced by special-interest groups will to a great extent be concerned with the provision of public goods and will usually impose only relatively tolerable losses in economic efficiency upon an economy. Really large distortions in the economy will usually arise only because of the lobbying or cartelization by narrow special-interest organizations.

We can therefore test whether the theory fits the facts by looking at the experience of the market democracies of the West. If my theory is right, we should expect that societies that set up a good legal order, after a catastrophe has destroyed organizations for collective action, will, for a time, grow extraordinarily rapidly. Similarly, societies that have been stable for a long time ought to grow much less rapidly than societies that are in other respects comparable.

The society that has had the longest period of stability and immunity from invasion and institutional destruction is Great Britain. As the theory predicts, Great Britain also has had the "British disease"—the poorest economic performance of the major developed democracies. The economic miracles of Germany and Japan after World War II are also consistent with the argument. With appropriate elaboration, the aforementioned theory also explains the general pattern of regional growth in the United States since World War II. Most of the tests and evaluations by others are corroborative.[4]

Economic Growth in Autocracies and Democracies

If the arguments in Chapter 2 are right, many autocrats have short time horizons and thus have little more concern for the productivity of their societies than a transient bandit, and the only societies that will have secure property and contract rights across generations are lasting democracies or other representative governments. If the arguments in Chapter 1 and earlier in this chapter are right, autocrats have, by the standards of special-interest groups that represent particular industries, occupations, or professions, relatively encompassing stakes in the societies they rule (though definitely less encompassing stakes than majorities).

Though the observed pattern of economic growth could also be consistent with other theories, it is certainly consistent with the theory offered here. Capital often flees from autocratic, often autocratic, or temporarily democratic societies (even though capital is relatively scarce in these societies and should have a good return) to lasting democracies (even though they are relatively well supplied with capital and do not offer high returns). Thus, the extraordinarily unequal distribution of capital across the countries of the world is strikingly consistent with the argument in Chapter 2, as is the usually mediocre and sometimes disastrous economic performance in most societies with autocracy, whether in recent times or in earlier history.

At the same time, there has not only been net long-term growth of output and population over long autocratic historical epochs but also impressive recent economic growth under a number of strong, secure, and relatively well-advised autocrats. Extensive statistical work that my colleagues and I have done on about a hundred countries shows that there is a

strong, significant, and robust relationship between the time
an autocrat has been in office and the quality of property and
contract rights in his domain.[5] There has also been spectacu-
lar growth under a few autocrats (such as in Taiwan, South
Korea, Singapore, China, and Chile) in relatively recent times.
The economically most successful autocrats not only tend to
have long planning horizons but also to resist or repress
special-interest groups: they tend to have "hard" states that
do not usually adapt their policies to organized interests in
particular occupations or industries. Though a complete account of experience in any country would require taking
account of the many important considerations that are left
out of the theory offered here, the overall pattern is very much
in accord with the theory.

6

THE SOURCES OF LAW
ENFORCEMENT AND
CORRUPTION

There is one logical possibility that could make the theory in Chapters 1 and 2 wrong, which it is important to analyze (even though no one is likely to think that, in practice, it could invalidate the argument) because it brings a new point of great practical importance to our attention. This possibility is that the costs of protecting all the assets in a domain from theft and providing other essential public goods could conceivably exceed a government's maximum possible tax collections. We noted in the analysis of anarchy in Chapter 3 that a family in an anarchic environment might rationally devote more time to protecting what it has against theft than to production. When government takes on responsibility for law and order, could this be comparably expensive? Neither a king nor a democratic government can know of every sparrow's fall in a country, and the police needed to keep watch on all of the assets in a country, plus the courts, prisons, and other collective goods that go with them, could be prohibitively expensive.

In fact, the costs of providing law and order should be—and for many countries are—simply trivial in relation to tax collections and the national income. We know that providing a peaceful order and other essential goods need not cost much in relation to tax receipts: many autocrats extract huge surpluses for their own aggressions and other extravagances, and most democratic governments engage in vast amounts of discretionary spending (that is, spending not necessary for law and order and the viability of democratic government). Yet in most of the third world—and in the former Soviet Union as well as some other formerly communist countries—there are huge "informal" sectors in which much of the population lives outside of the law out of necessity. They also suffer pervasive corruption in government. When we understand why the costs of providing law and order and other public goods needed for governmental viability can be relatively trivial, we will have a new and better comprehension of official corruption, crime, and why some countries have large shadow economies or informal sectors.

There are two major reasons why it need not cost much to maintain law and order. The first reason is evident when we think about the sources of violence and other costly conflict. If parties who might engage in a costly conflict know each other's relative strengths, and both agree that one party is vastly stronger than the other, they almost never fight. Both sides know how a battle would turn out, so both know that they can gain from agreeing to a solution that saves them the costs of the conflict. The settlement normally takes account of the disparity in strength; the weaker party gives ground to the stronger. By contrast, when the parties are of similar strength, it is much more likely that one party will be wrong about the relative strength of the other and mistakenly expect to obtain a better outcome by threatening to fight than by accepting the terms of the other. That is one reason why people regularly flee areas of anarchy and move, even (when necessary) to places that are exploitively and badly governed.

When an individual such as an autocrat has established himself—or when a democratic government has established a police force—the power of the government is incomparably greater than that of a subject or citizen. Once it is clear that this is the case, the government normally no longer needs to bear much cost from fighting its subjects; they know their best choice is not to challenge the government.

This point is not new: it was eloquently made, for the special case of autocratic government, by Thomas Hobbes. He advocated an autocrat whose power was so great that all subjects were utterly overawed. Hobbes believed that such an autocrat was necessary to ensure a peaceful order.

The second reason why it need not be costly for a government to maintain a peaceful order is that it can, by adopting the right public policies and institutions, count on powerful private-sector incentives to greatly reinforce the government's efforts at law enforcement and to bear much of the costs of maintaining law and order in the private sector. Consider the private-sector incentives to prevent crime and to induce law-abiding behavior that exist in societies with good economic policies and institutions. The self-interest of the individuals and firms in a market economy with good economic policies and clearly delineated property rights is a major force for crime prevention, lawful behavior, and law enforcement.

Consider the prevention of theft or the maintenance of property rights. The self-interest of owners leads them to guard against theft. The interests of individuals and firms leads them to install locks, hide valuables, hire guards, and keep watch. Admittedly, individuals and firms in societies with ambiguous property rights, and even those (as we saw in Chapter 3) in anarchic conditions, have a similar interest in avoiding being the victims of theft. In societies with well-defined property rights, however, the theft-averting activities that individuals and private firms undertake in their own interest reinforce and strengthen the law and make it less expensive for the government to enforce the law.

The self-interest of individuals and firms in the private sector often helps the police, the courts, and the government in apprehending and punishing theft. When a family or a firm is the victim of a theft, they normally report the offense to the police and provide whatever information they can to help the government apprehend the thief. Sometimes firms and individuals will also offer rewards for information that leads to the apprehension of criminals who prey upon them.

There is, admittedly, also the self-interest of thieves. The thief has an incentive to conceal his crime and avoid apprehension, and sometimes even to bribe the police or the judge. The self-interest of criminals works everywhere to undermine the law. Yet, in a market economy with good institutions and economic policies, there are always, on the other side, the victims and potential victims of crime who not only use locks and hide valuables but report offenses, pressure the police to recover stolen property, and testify against offenders.

Pressure to Uphold the Law

The fact that (when there are good institutions and economic policies) private self-interest limits crime and corruption is, when looked at closely, much more important than it first appears. Consider the cost of enforcing laws against fraud. Though the police and the courts are important in deterring fraud, surely the wariness of the individuals and firms who do not want to be cheated is also crucial. So long as a government has the policy of buyer beware, governments do not need to spend much to combat fraud.

Consider also the enforcement of loan contracts. Suppose that somebody who has borrowed money decides not to pay it back. The borrower has an incentive to work against the enforcement of the loan contract, but the lender will try to induce the borrower to pay the loan back by threatening his reputation and access to future credit and, if necessary, by petitioning the courts to seize the borrower's assets. Because lenders, in deciding to whom to lend, favor borrowers with the lowest risks, a higher proportion of loans are paid back than if lenders did not exercise this judgment. That, of course, makes repayment of loans more common and generates a habitual obedience to the private law that grows out of a mutually agreed contract.

Consider also the differences in the power and wealth of people and firms in the private sector. Usually, in a successful market economy, the same inequalities in wealth and power that are, in other respects, a problem, help to maintain law and order. When theft and the enforcement of contracts are at issue, the more substantial and wealthier interests will normally be on the side of upholding the law. If the average burglar is not as prosperous or politically influential as his victim, the net force of the private sector is on the side of the law. If lenders are on average more influential than borrowers, loan contract enforcement works better. It also helps those who can gain from borrowing money by creating an environment where money can be borrowed on reasonable terms. The net private force in support of many laws is, I think, a matter of extraordinary importance.

As we shall see later, the situation is dramatically different in societies with bad economic policies and poor institutions. But the pertinent point at the moment is that governments with decent institutions and policies can maintain sufficient law and order for economic progress at relatively low costs because of the self-interest of private parties. When we combine this point with the idea that majorities have encompassing stakes in society that give them an interest in productivity that limits redistribution to themselves, we obtain a fairly optimistic perspective on modern democratic societies. The encompassing majorities that control these societies have an incentive to choose good economic policies and institutions; then they can obtain a reasonable degree of law and order at modest costs.

Unanimous Private-Sector Pressure
Against Enforcement

Now let us look at countries that do not have good economic policies and institutions. Suppose that the government fixes prices and sets a price lower than the market-clearing price. The quantity demanded will be higher than the quantity that the suppliers, at the lower-than-market-clearing price, want to supply. It will then be the case that there can be a mutually advantageous trade—one with both a buyer and a seller gaining—at a price that is higher than the controlled price and lower than the market-clearing price. Both parties gain by violating the law, and, in dramatic contrast to violations of the law on private property, neither has an incentive to report the offense. Essentially all of the private-sector incentive is to undermine the law. Of course, the same thing holds true if the government sets a price above market-clearing levels.

Now suppose that the government determines how much of a good will be produced and that the quantity chosen by the planners is lower than the quantity that the market would have generated. There will be some buyers who do not get as much as they would like and some potential sellers who would profit from supplying these buyers at a price they are willing to pay. Both parties can gain from evading the law and, if necessary, corrupting the officials who are supposed to enforce it.

Assume that it is ordained by the government that a good must be produced in excess of the amount that the market would dictate, or that a good must be produced that the market would not produce at all. There are enormous costs that producers can escape if they do not produce this good or do not produce the prescribed amount of it, and (since the production is by stipulation uneconomic) the good is not worth nearly as much to buyers, so they do not put up much of a fight for it. The general point is that legislation or regulation that is *market contrary* must leave all or almost all parties with the incentive to evade the law, and it is likely to promote criminality and corruption in government.

Thus, one reason why many societies have a lot of corruption in government is that they prescribe outcomes that all or almost all private parties have an incentive to avoid, and no one in the private sector has an incentive to report violations to the authorities. Moreover, when caught in violation of the rule, those on both sides of the market have the same incentive to persuade or bribe the officials not to enforce the law. Essentially all of the private-sector incentives are on the side of undermining the rules. Sooner or later, the government becomes corrupt and ineffective.

The governments of the third world attempt to impose incomparably more market-contrary policies than do the governments of the prosperous market economies. As the forgoing argument predicts, they also have vastly more corruption in their governments. The huge informal economies in the third world are evidence not only of the extent of market-contrary policies but of the extent to which these policies have led over time to the corruption and ineffectiveness of third-world governments.

Market-contrary activity was, of course, also the norm in the communist countries. As many people who lived under communism testify, in the Soviet-type countries sometimes a factory manager could not even get his work done—could not fulfill his quota—without engaging in quasi-legal or illegal deals to obtain inputs. The whole system of Soviet-style planning was so market-contrary that even the high officials—and perhaps especially the high officials—had to violate the rules and the plan in order to comply with the orders and targets they were given. That is, the market-contrary activity often stood in the way of achieving some of the objectives of the regime.

We now have a part of the explanation for the chorus of complaints about crime and official corruption in the East, but only a part. As we shall see, we greatly understate the extent to which Soviet-type arrangements undermined law-abiding behavior and the integrity of government officials by saying that the Soviet-type societies restricted private property and markets to an unprecedented degree. The type of system that Stalin initiated had a more fundamental feature that prompted even more illicit activity and official corruption than could be accounted for by the foregoing argument.

We not only need to explain why corruption increased so much over the life of the communist system (and why it is a serious problem for the postcommunist societies) but also other features of Soviet-type systems and the difficulties of transition. It turns out that the theory that has been developed in this book can, with some parsimonious extensions, provide a totally new perspective on the type of system that Stalin created and on the difficulties of the transition to democratic societies with market economies. We start on this new perspective in the next chapter.

7

THE THEORY OF
SOVIET-TYPE AUTOCRACIES

THE THEORY OF AUTOCRACY discussed in Chapters 1 and 2 puts the spotlight on two reasons why the Soviet Union was for a time thought to offer both an economic and a military challenge to the United States and its allies. The Soviet Union was an autocracy and therefore (1) it was governed by an encompassing interest—the more productive the Soviet domain was, other things being equal, the more resources were available to achieve the autocrat's objectives, so the First Secretary of the Communist party had a powerful incentive to make the society more productive; (2) its leader extracted the largest possible surplus from the society to increase his political power, military might, and international influence.

Though these factors are important, they do not explain why communist autocracies are communist. Until Stalin consolidated his control over the Soviet political system, no autocrat had ever organized his domain the way Stalin organized the Soviet Union. Why did Stalin impose on the Soviet Union (and later on the satellite countries) an economic system with almost universal state ownership and a large proportion of prices and wages set by the regime?

The conventional assumption—that the choice for a centrally planned economy was because of Marxist-Leninist ideology—is inadequate. Saying that the actions of autocrats are explained by their ideologies adds only a word rather than an explanation unless we explain what inspired that ideology and why an autocrat chose that ideology rather than some other doctrinal or eclectic alternative. When a power-hungry autocrat is trying to gain power and he espouses an ideology that is popular with the constituency or power base that he has to win over, we have an explanation of his use of that ideology. Thus, when Stalin was struggling to win dictatorial control over the USSR, it is not surprising that in the early 1920's he joined the apparently stronger or pivotal faction that (like Lenin himself) had opted for the market-oriented New Economic Policy and had decided against the forced collectivization of agriculture.

After he obtained unchallenged power, Stalin did not need to please any Bolshevik faction, and he then adopted policies that he had previously opposed: total state absorption of the economy with brutal collectivization of agriculture. It does not add much to say that this was done for unexplained ideological reasons, especially when Stalin was not a consistent adherent to a single ideological position. Marx's writings also did not require the economic organization that Stalin imposed; Marx had focused on capitalism and said almost nothing about the organization of socialist or communist societies. In time, because of Stalin's practice and propaganda, Marxist-Leninist ideology came to be identified with the type of economic and political system he had imposed, but this later rationalization cannot explain the choices Stalin made when he initially obtained dictatorial power.

Especially in view of the inadequacy of existing explanations of the special economic system in the communist autocracies, we need to extend the general theory of autocracy presented in Chapters 1 and 2 so that it can elucidate the special economic system in the communist autocracies.

The Limits on Autocratic Extraction

What limits the amount of resources that an autocrat can extract from his society? As was shown earlier, the rational autocrat, in contrast to the individual criminal in a populous society, does not take all of the money in the till. Given his encompassing interest, he keeps reducing his tax-theft rate from that confiscatory level down to the point where what he gains, because a lower rate increases output and the tax base, is just offset by what he loses, because he obtains a smaller share of output—this leaves him at the revenue-maximizing tax rate. Is there anything he can do to obtain still more? One possibility is the confiscation of the capital of his subjects. Another possibility is that the autocrat can start taxing real money balances by printing money for his own use in such amounts that unexpected inflation results. Another alternative is that he can borrow money and then refuse to pay it back.

As we know from Chapter 2, whenever an autocrat has a short enough time horizon these possibilities can serve his interests. The autocrat who expects to be around for a long time, by contrast, will normally lose from confiscation, inflation, and repudiation of his debts. I hypothesize that Stalin, at least after he consolidated his power in the late 1920s, expected to be in office (as he was) until he died a natural death. For the most part, he did not engage in inflationary methods to obtain resources and he scrupulously paid off the sums he borrowed from Western firms. In these respects, he was typical of intelligent autocrats who have a long time horizon. Autocrats with a long time horizon usually cannot gain from confiscating capital assets, because it normally means that there will be less investment and less income, and therefore smaller tax receipts, in the future.

Thus, it appears that expropriation of capital goods, because it reduces future investment and income, cannot increase the tax receipts of an autocrat over the long run. But there is one way that it can, and Stalin and his henchmen, evidently by trial and error, were the first to discover this way.

Confiscations That Increase
Savings and Investment

Stalin confiscated all of the farmland and natural resources of the Soviet Union, and all of the commercial and industrial property that had been privately held in the period of the New Economic Policy, and the Soviet Union's rate of savings and investment increased greatly. In general, after Stalin's innovation the Soviet Union and the other societies on which the Stalinist system was imposed had far higher rates of savings and investment than most other societies. Stalin's innovation was to confiscate for his own purposes almost the total natural and tangible capital stock of the country and then to use these resources to produce a mix of output that was much more intensive in capital goods and other goods Stalin wanted than would otherwise have been produced.

By determining himself how much of the nation's resources would be used to produce consumer goods, and keeping this proportion much smaller than it was in most other societies, Stalin gave the Soviet Union an extraordinarily high rate of capital accumulation at the same time that he augmented his annual tax receipts by an amount approximately equal to all rent, interest, and profits—all nonlabor income. Stalin continued to receive more golden eggs than ever, even after he had killed the goose.[1] In the long history of stationary banditry, no prior autocrat seems to have managed this task.

How Taxes Can Increase the Incentive to Work

However unconsciously or accidentally, Stalin and his accomplices also came upon a second innovation in tax collection. Most of Stalin's resources were obtained by a special system of implicit taxation—by taking all of the profits of state-owned enterprises rather than explicitly taxing individuals.

Stalin had the subordinates he put in charge of the economy set wages and salaries very low, and establish prices for most consumer goods that were (in relation to these minimal rates of pay) relatively high. As Ronald McKinnon's important work on this subject has explained,[2] the main sources of tax revenue for the Soviet-type societies were the profits of industrial enterprises (and turnover taxes that, given the prices set by the planners, were mainly taxes on the profits of these enterprises). Thus, Stalin not only claimed for the regime all of the profits of state enterprises (which included, as we know from the preceding section, essentially all of the natural resource rents and interest or return to capital in the society) but he had his planners set wage rates and consumer prices at levels that would make these sums—and therfore implicit taxes—exceptionally high. (This was not the case in late Soviet times, but we are looking first at the system that Stalin set up and will deal with its devolution over time later.)

When wages and salaries were set very low, people could not afford much leisure. Everyone had to enter the labor force, including huge numbers of women who had not been working before. To fix ideas and to see the logical essence of the system as simply as possible, think of the base rates of pay as set below the level of subsistence. Of course, if this were the whole of the story, the labor force would not have survived, national output would have fallen, and Stalin's tax collections would have decreased.

But consider the second feature of this system of implicit taxation: little or no implicit taxation on extra, overtime, above-the-norm, or "bonus" work and productivity. Stalin used, for example, progressive piece rates—that is, piece rates that increased the per-unit payment with the amount that the person produced. There is also piece work in democracies with market economies, but not usually progressive piece rates. If you are picking fruit or selling insurance policies, you might be paid by the bushel picked or by the policy sold. But you are not paid progressively higher rates per unit for higher amounts for the obvious reason that this usually would not be an efficient contract for a typical employer and a typical employee to make.[3]

Stalin's combination of bonuses, progressive piece rates, prizes for Stakhanovites, and special perquisites for other especially productive workers provided people with a large proportion of the marginal or overtime output that they produced, but at the same time implicitly taxed them very highly on their inframarginal work. The effect of the virtually confiscatory rate of tax on the normal amount of work and little or no taxation of extra or bonus income is that the taxation increases the incentive to work.

Why a Larger Income and Smaller Substitution Effect Must Increase the Incentive to Work

In Figure 7.1 leisure is measured along the horizontal axis and consumption is measured along the vertical axis. Let us suppose for simplicity that we have a linear or flat tax and that the rate of this tax has been set, on traditional autocratic principles, at the revenue-maximizing rate. Let us further assume that this also happens to leave the worker in question at the subsistence level. The total output of the individual is given by the pretax wage curve in the figure. Instead of getting the full value of his or her output, the individual gets the much lower revenue-maximizing posttax wage depicted in Figure 7.1. In the case shown, the individual chooses the amount of leisure OLF and he or she obtains OA of money income. The autocrat obtains amount AB as tax receipts.

How did Stalin improve on this simple and straightforward autocratic optimum? He set the person's wage or salary at very low levels and captured most of the value of the individual's output during the ordinary working day in implicit taxation—by keeping the profits of state enterprises (and especially industrial enterprises), which were made far higher than they would otherwise have been because wages were set so low.

If taken to the polar extreme, this person is faced with a lump-sum tax of CD = EF, but this individual is not taxed on marginal income. As a result, the individual will, of course, take less leisure. He cannot afford much leisure because of the high tax rate and he receives a greater reward for additional hours of work because there is no taxation of marginal income. This individual under the Stalinist mode of taxation will take an amount of leisure OLD, which will lead to much higher out-

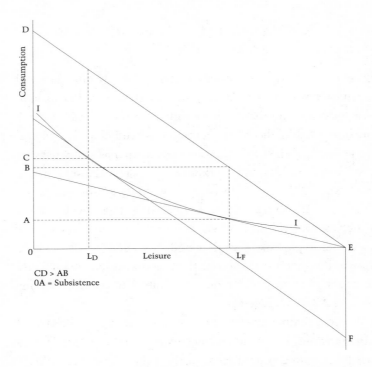

FIGURE 7.1 ◆ Autocratic Maximization with Lump-Sum Taxation

put. In this case, the state will obtain CD of output—much more than was obtained by ordinary autocratic taxation at the revenue-maximizing rate. The individual gets the same level of utility as before (and more consumption), but the dictator gets much more revenue; with indifference curves (iso-utility lines) of the normal shape, CD necessarily is larger than AB.

Let us further suppose that OA is the subsistence level. If Stalin's system of making inframarginal tax rates higher and marginal tax rates lower (or zero) is used, it is possible to take still more than CD in taxes. Indeed, if we go to the extreme of assuming that the regime knows exactly what the productive potential of the individual is and also knows just how much the worker needs for subsistence, then the regime can choose a lump-sum tax that takes everything that the worker can produce above the subsistence level, yet also has the worker providing much more labor than he would have supplied had he faced a flat tax or no tax at all. Of course, the outcome was not this extreme, and we will consider more realistic cases in the next two sections.

Maximizing Tax Collections with Differences in Abilities

If an autocrat has different tax schedules for individuals of different productivities, he can collect much more tax revenue than if the same tax brackets apply to everyone. In the typical modern democracy, high-income people confront higher tax rates or brackets than do low-income people, but everyone faces the same tax law or schedule.

When everyone faces the same tax schedule, it is impossible to tax people more on their first hours of work than on their marginal hours of work and also to have very high tax rates. Obviously, if we were taxed heavily on the first four hours a day of work, less on the next two, and not at all on hours after that, then we would have an incentive to work a lot more. We would have a stronger incentive to work because, if we were taxed heavily enough on the first few hours of work, we would be poorer and the *income effect* of taxation would make us work more. If we were not taxed on our last hours of work, we would also have a greater posttax reward for additional work, so a larger *substitution effect* would make us work more. Economic efficiency would increase. So in some sense the Western democracies would be more efficient and productive if it were possible for us to be taxed more on our first hours of work, but not taxed on our last or marginal hours of work.

But that's not a real possibility when we all face the same tax schedule. Suppose that the United States decided to tax the first $5,000 a person makes a year at 99 percent, the next $5,000 at 98 percent, and so forth, and to tax what each person makes above a certain level at zero percent. This method—reversing the usual progression and regressively taxing lower incomes at much higher rates than higher incomes—would create a situation where the least productive people would not have even enough income to survive. The productivity and efficiency-enhancing policy of taxing people more on their first hours of work—or, more generally, on their inframarginal income—but not taxing their marginal income, is not only morally repugnant but practically impossible when the same laws apply to everyone.

There is, however, a way that a cunning autocrat can extract most of the greater surplus above subsistence needs that the more able can produce and, at the same time, also extract all or most of the surplus over subsistence produced by those who have less productive potential. Somehow, Stalin and his advisers hit upon this method and he was power-hungry and ruthless enough to put it into practice. The method is to set the basic or inframarginal wage or salary of each occupation and ability level in the society with the purpose of collecting the maximum income for the autocrat's purposes from those in each occupation and ability level.

All that is needed is to set the base or inframarginal wage of those in the jobs that require more ability at almost the same level as those of unskilled workers. A far higher implicit tax rate is put on the more able people in the more productive roles. Only the tiniest premiums, if any, are needed to provide an incentive for the more able people to accept the jobs that require higher ability, because the system of placing little or no tax on marginal or "bonus" income means that the more productive are able to keep most of their higher output for extra work.

A Schematic Presentation

Figure 7.2 depicts a system for two individuals in jobs that require different levels of ability, on the assumption that the regime could literally have a lump-sum tax. Again, OA gives the level of consumption that each individual needs for subsistence. The less talented individual's (the unskilled worker's) total output is given by the line FC and the more talented individual's (the manager's) total output is given by the line FE. The autocrat, by setting the rates of pay in each job far below the level of productivity, but by leaving the marginal pay virtually untaxed, approximately achieves the effect of a lump-sum or head tax. By taxing the inframarginal pay in the more demanding and productive job more heavily than the less demanding job—that is, by making the differential in the basic or inframarginal wage much lower than the productivity differential of the two types of work—the autocrat can obtain most of the larger surplus above subsistence needs that the more able individual produces.

The tax on the manager is DE = FH, while the tax on the worker is BC = FG. The manager, if he has the same preference ordering as the worker, necessarily finds it in his interest to take even less leisure than the worker at the subsistence level. The only thing that keeps the autocrat from taking all of the surplus above consumption produced by the more able individual is the imperfection of the regime's knowledge of the exact ability or potential productivity level of the more able individual. As this knowledge improves, the autocrat can obtain more of the surplus above subsistence produced by the more able worker.

In fact, the regime did not have a lump-sum tax and had only a rough idea of the potential productivity of different individuals. But it knew which jobs required higher abilities. It imposed a two-part wage in the form of a very low basic wage, making

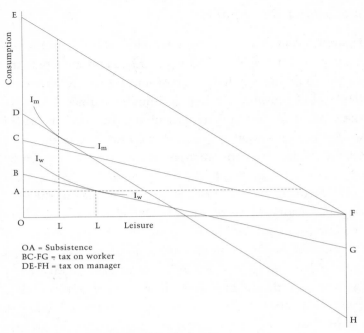

FIGURE 7.2 ◆ Tax-Price Discrimination

this basic wage only slightly higher for jobs that demanded great ability than for unskilled work. In jobs that required high skill and those that did not, there was little or no tax on marginal income. The regime set the wage for the lowest skill of labor so low that, even with no tax on marginal income, workers at this lower level of skill earned only approximately a subsistence income, with the regime taking all the rest of their productivity. This situation of the less productive worker is depicted in Figure 7.3.

For jobs that required greater ability and had higher productivity, the regime set a basic wage that was only slightly higher,

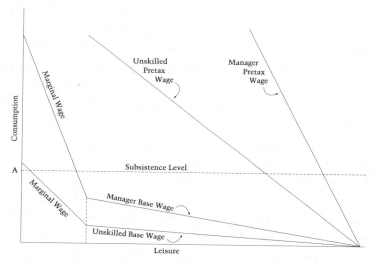

FIGURE 7.3 ◆ Two-Part Wage with Discrimination

but let the more able person keep all or nearly all of his or her marginal or bonus income. This situation for the more productive worker is also depicted in Figure 7.3. Though the regime captures much of the larger surplus above subsistence produced by the more able worker, it cannot get it all. In order to provide incentives for the more able people to take the more productive jobs and to work harder at those jobs, the regime must let them receive all or most of their marginal output, which is so high that it ensures that they will end up with a higher-than-subsistence level of consumption.

From Each According to His Ability, to the Man in Charge

The small differentials in base or prebonus pay across occupations in Stalin's Soviet Union were sometimes said to be motivated by egalitarian ideology. In fact, Stalin set egalitarian ideals aside to maximize the incentive to produce—he was explicit and emphatic about this. The extra effort of the people in the most important and demanding jobs was elicited by having very low taxes on their marginal income—the bonuses, the allocation of housing, the distribution of scarce consumption goods at the workplace, the prizes for Stakhanovites, and so on—and by keeping all inframarginal incomes so low that people could afford relatively little leisure. If an egalitarian ethic had been driving the system, the implicit taxes for the purposes of the autocrat would not have been so large and there would have been no progressive piece rates or other devices that made marginal income especially unequal.

Stalin said explicitly that there should be inequalities in pay to improve incentives and these inequalities did, in fact, exist. As we have seen, so long as marginal tax rates were zero or very low, Stalin needed only small differentials in inframarginal rates of pay: the more able individual could earn much more in bonuses and other forms of marginal pay if he were in a job where he could be more highly productive than he could at a humbler job. With wages and salaries that provided only austere levels of consumption, the higher marginal earnings in the more demanding jobs were made all the more attractive. In a job with higher productivity, the more able person also had an incentive to work harder than the less able person, since with low taxes on marginal income he would have a higher posttax reward for his marginal hours of work.

Therefore, the system of taxation that collects the most revenue meets two conditions. First, it confronts more productive people with different implicit tax schedules than those applied to less productive people. Second, given that the first condition is met, it is possible (even with very high tax rates) to tax inframarginal income more highly than marginal income. The familiar Western progressive income tax does not meet these conditions at all. Thus, it is no coincidence that the Soviet Union, even as it attacked the market democracies for their inequalities of income, did not in any serious way use the progressive income tax. For a long time, the maximum rate of income tax in the Soviet Union, for example, was only 13 percent.

To prevent the managers and workers of state enterprises from obtaining any of the autocrat's implicit tax receipts, interenterprise payments had to be made through the state banking system; enterprises were normally not allowed to keep anything more than petty cash. Payments in cash, such as wages of workers, were handed out by the state banks rather than by the enterprises. The expenditures of enterprises out of bank accounts were, moreover, limited by the planning officials. (This system changed as the Soviet-type countries aged, but that is a topic that must be left to the next chapter.)

We have explained the paradox that the degree of income inequality of the Stalinist system was restricted, and the proportion of income taken in taxes was uniquely high, but the incentive to work was greater than would be expected from the high rate of taxation and the limited degree of inequality. The highly egalitarian inframarginal pay rates, and the lightly taxed or untaxed marginal earnings, are precisely the conditions that maximize tax collections. To paraphrase an old saying, it was "from each according to his ability, to the man in charge."

The proportion of income in the Soviet Union in Stalin's time that was devoted to personal consumption was lower than in virtually any noncommunist country, and that is exactly what the theory here predicts. Stalin was able to obtain a larger proportion of the national output for his own purposes than any other government in history was able to extract.

Socialism Versus Extraction in Agriculture

The origins of Stalin's innovative system of tax collection showed up most starkly in agriculture. The Soviet Union was mainly an agricultural country when the Bolsheviks took over in 1917. Most of the national income was produced in agriculture, and especially by the *kulaks*—those with larger farms. Thus, there was no way that the Bolsheviks could obtain a large part of the Soviet national income for their own purposes unless they could get their hands on most of the output produced in the rural areas, which posed a major problem for them. Most notably, they had to have a surplus of grain to feed their cadre, who were mainly in the cities. They also needed more people in the cities to man factories and to produce steel and armaments, and more people in the military and government bureaucracy to do the work of the regime. So the Soviets wanted more food and could only obtain it from the peasants and kulaks.

In order to have the resources needed to build heavy industry and produce armaments, and to supply the party cadre and the army, the Bolsheviks first offered low prices to food producers, thereby implicitly putting a high tax on the kulaks and the peasants. Of course, the response of the farmers was to produce less, to consume more of what they produced at home, and to sell food privately and illegally. The only way the Bolsheviks could have obtained the food they needed would have been to pay the farmers enough to give them an incentive to produce more. But that would have used up much of the social surplus that the regime wanted to devote to industrialization, to the military, and to political and prestige projects. So the Bolsheviks had to work out a collection system that would get more of a taxable surplus out of the agricultural sector, which was then the main part of the Soviet economy.

Before Stalin had consolidated his power, some of the more "radical" Bolsheviks argued that the Soviet Union needed "primitive socialist accumulation." This was the socialist analogue to Marx's "primitive capitalist accumulation"—the initial thefts and windfalls to which Marx had attributed the capitalists' initial accumulation of capital. Some Bolsheviks argued, by analogy with Marxian economic theory, that there was no alternative but to take the initial capital needed for socialist industrialization from the kulaks and the peasants. Though Stalin at first aligned himself with the moderate Bolsheviks who opposed such a seizure, he adopted the radical program as soon as he had consolidated his power.

He then confiscated the agricultural land, livestock, and machinery of the country, imposing extraordinarily severe punishments on peasants who hid grain or livestock. He dealt especially harshly with the kulaks, who had the greatest reason to resist. Those assigned to each collective farm were made responsible for providing a given amount of grain or other foodstuffs to the state. Stalin set up the system in such a way that monitoring was facilitated so that the implicit taxes could not usually be evaded. Separate organizations providing tractor services to the collective farms and Communist party units helped prevent collective farms from escaping the implicit tax. Thus, Stalin's system was designed to make it easier to determine the amount that people had to supply to the state and thus to tax them as much as they were capable of being taxed.

I submit, then, that the collective farm was mainly an instrument of tax collection, not something that was ideologically required. The ideologically preferred system of organization was the state farm, where the workers were paid a wage and the state was the residual claimant. But in state farms much of the output was taken up in wages paid to the workers, so these farms did not provide much surplus for the regime. Thus, Stalin chose collective farms and made the members of the collective farms responsible for supplying the amounts (the theoretical "biological yield") he demanded: the collective farms could not keep the resources needed to pay state farm wages to their members. Unlike state farms, collective farms seem to have been organized for "collections," not for "collectivist" governance.

After providing extensive labor services to the collective farm, the farmers were allowed to use leisure time for work on the tiny private plots that were allocated to them. As the theory here predicts, the income from these plots was not, in general, taxed.

From Stalin's point of view, the food collection system worked. During World War I, the Tsarist state (even though at times it used coercive measures to collect food) was not able to provide enough food to people in the cities to maintain its control: the February revolution began as a protest over the shortage of bread. By contrast, during World War II, the Soviet regime

had at its disposal a well-developed procurement system. . . . Despite a disastrous fall in food production per head of the collective farm population, the share of total meat and grain output taken by the government rose. The collective farmer was left with a reduced share of a smaller total than before the war. Even before the war the government attitude to the consumer needs of the farm population had been harsh and arbitrary. . . .

Military style procurement campaigns meant that the confiscation of food from farm stocks became still more arbitrary in wartime.[4]

In summary, Stalin's brutal and cunning innovations enabled his regime to:

1. Expropriate essentially all of the national stock of tangible capital, land, and other natural resources, thereby adding the yield of all of these assets each year to his tax collections.
2. Avoid the collapse of investment that normally follows such expropriation by directly controlling the level of consumption and investment, thereby giving the Soviet Union a far higher rate of saving and investment than other societies.
3. Raise taxes on labor income far above what had, under prior tax-collecting methods, been revenue-maximizing rates, partly by introducing tax-price discrimination that captured a larger part of the output of relatively productive individuals.
4. Reduce the ratio of marginal to average tax rates, thereby increasing not only the proportion of labor income paid in taxes but the amount of labor supplied both through the income effect (families could afford less leisure and home-produced output, so almost all women had to work outside the home) and the substitution effect (increasing the reward for marginal effort).

By the time that this system had been perfected, the Soviet Union had more resources for the purposes of the leadership than any other society in history.

Ideology as Smokescreen

Though Stalin was often considered the pope of Marxist religion, he was not, in fact, a sincere ideologue. Ideology no doubt
played a role in explaining some of his support, but the hypothesis here is that Stalin was not blinded by—or even faithful
to—what had previously been called Marxism. If Stalin had
been a committed ideologue, he would not have killed off all
the people who had participated with him as initial leaders of
the Bolshevik revolution, or purged those Bolsheviks who dared
to defend their Marxist principles, or made the Nazi-Soviet
pact. Stalin also did nothing to bring about the withering of the
state that Marx had predicted and advocated.

Yet he did a great deal to increase the size and power of the
Soviet military and the industrial and scientific base that it required. Though the main features of the Stalinist system were
not required by Marx's writings or by Lenin's example in the
period of the somewhat market-oriented New Economic
Policy, they are consistent with the hypothesis that Stalin
wanted, above all else, the power that increased tax collections could give him.

A Test: The Ratio of Power to Income

The foregoing theory is consistent with the history of Soviet-
type societies and, unlike the assertion that the Soviet type of
economic organization was due to ideology, it offers an analysis with genuine explanatory power. More than one theory
can, however, be consistent with the historical facts and also
meaningful, so we must ask what implications of the theory
offered here would expose it to further testing.

If the theory is true, the military or geopolitical power and
the expenditures on projects that add to the status and pres-

tige of political leaders should have been greater, in relation to the standard of living of the population, than in other societies—even other autocratic societies. A casual glance at the historical record is enough to show that this was the case.

There have been many noncommunist dictatorships that offer instructive comparisons with communist countries. Since World War II, for example, there have been many dictatorships, especially in Latin America and Africa, that were not communist. But none of these other dictatorships has been remotely as formidable or influential as the Soviet Union or communist China. Most other autocracies did not, to be sure, preside over such large domains or such huge populations as the USSR or communist China came to control. But this is not in many cases sufficient to explain why they were not as formidable.

Tsarist Russia, though the largest country on earth, was not able to give a good account of itself in the Crimean War. Nor was it even able to defeat in 1904–5 the only semimodern island society of Japan at that time. Similarly, Chiang Kai-shek's China, though it had the world's largest population, was militarily impotent.

Compare also tsarist Russia in World War I with Stalin's USSR. In World War I, the gigantic empire of the tsars was defeated essentially only by Germany,[5] even though the German army had its hands full fighting on a second front against the French and British from the beginning of the war and normally used only a small fraction of its forces against Russia. By contrast, in World War II, Stalin's Soviet Union was victorious against Nazi Germany, even though the Germans committed the great bulk of their fighting troops to the Soviet front: there was no "second front" until the Normandy invasion in June 1944. Though German ground and air munitions production was 2.6 times as large in World War II as in World War I, Soviet munitions production was 24.5 times as high in World War II as the Russian Empire's munitions production in World War I.[6]

Whatever interpretation may be offered for the fortunes of the different Russian autocracies in World Wars I and II, there can be no doubt that after World War II the Soviet Union was universally accorded a superpower status that the tsarist autocracy never achieved. The tsars also never managed a prestige coup comparable to the Soviet initiation of flight in space.

When the Stalinist system was applied in China, Vietnam, and North Korea, it again made the communist autocracies incomparably more powerful militarily and politically than other third-world regimes. Communist China was never so inconsequential militarily as the autocracy it replaced. It was able (with North Korea) to fight the United States and its allies to a draw in the Korean War. There is also communist North Vietnam's feat in forcing the United States eventually to abandon its objectives in the Vietnam War. Part of the story is that the U.S. commitment to the Vietnam and Korean Wars was far from complete, that the United States was inhibited from using nuclear weapons, and so on. Still, when comparing the military and geopolitical significance of the communist regimes in China, North Korea, and North Vietnam with preceding regimes and with other third-world countries with similarly abysmal standards of living, my theory that the communist economies were unprecedentedly effective systems of resource mobilization or tax collection is surely supported.

The Inefficiency and Decline
of the Stalinist System

Having given the Stalinist devil its due, we must not forget the well-known point that the Soviet system, even at its best, was inefficient. The Soviet system mobilized a fantastic amount of resources, but it did not use these resources well. Stalin's confiscations eliminated many of the markets needed for an efficient economy. To obtain all of what would, in a market economy, have been interest, rent, and profit, Stalin confiscated the capital, land, and other natural resources of the Soviet Union and thereby eliminated the private asset and rental markets for these assets. In eliminating privately owned firms, he denied the society the gains from the innovations that private entrepreneurs would have made. By setting wage and salary levels and differentials administratively in order to obtain a larger share of labor income, Stalin also distorted labor markets, though by much less than expected because his taxation fell mainly on inframarginal earnings. As a result of the elimination and distortion of markets required for Stalin's system of resource mobilization or taxation, the total factor productivity of the Soviet-type societies was lower—and was growing less rapidly—than in market economies of comparable levels of development.

In the early years, Soviet societies achieved rapid economic growth, in spite of their slow growth of total factor productivity, because they had extraordinarily high rates of investment. These exceptional rates of saving and investment were, as I argued earlier, due in turn to the uniquely high proportion of national output that they captured. For about the first two decades after World War II, the societies that grew out of Stalin's innovations and conquests were able to make up for their inefficiency through their extraordinarily high savings and investment rates.

We already know that, as time went on, the Soviet-type societies began to stagnate. Though they continued with their high saving and investment, they were after a time unable to obtain even moderate productivity growth rates,[7] even though they still had a long way to go to catch up to Western levels.[8] Eventually, Soviet societies became severely sclerotic and, in time, they died.

How could a system that served Stalin so well—that made him arguably the most powerful individual in the world—become so sclerotic that it could not, in the long run, even survive? This was not a question that Stalin himself had to worry about. To paraphrase Keynes: In the long run, Stalin was dead. But it is a question that we must answer before we can know why the Soviet-type societies gradually deteriorated and ultimately collapsed. We also cannot understand why the transition from communism to democracy and a market economy has been so difficult—or how a postcommunist society can get through the transition and achieve Western levels of prosperity—without answering this question.

8

THE EVOLUTION
OF COMMUNISM AND
ITS LEGACY

THOUGH THE ROLE OF MARKETS in Soviet-type societies was much larger than is often supposed,[1] the Stalinist system obviously had to handle an awesome number of matters through its command and control system, and for this it had to rely on a vast army of nomenklatura and lesser administrators. How could the leadership of a Soviet-type economy—given that it had to make millions of decisions through a bureaucracy that in other societies are governed mainly by markets—obtain an even faintly rational allocation of resources? That such a system would be insensitive to consumer demands and would also have major inefficiencies is so well known that it does not require further discussion. But how could it work well enough to create and sustain a superpower?

I have explained how the encompassing interest of the Soviet dictator gave him a strong incentive to make his domain as productive as he could in the interest of increasing his total tax collections. We still need to explain how the autocrat was able to obtain the information, plans, and implementation of decisions from his bureaucracy that were needed to obtain a coherent allocation of resources. We must continue to keep track of the real intellectual challenge: How could such a system work at all?

Economists, operations researchers, and systems analysts have long understood theoretically what would be needed for a fully efficient planned economy. The leader of a communist society would need to have enterprise managers and other subordinates estimate the input-output possibilities or production functions of each and every enterprise and spell out the leader's objective function or goals in great detail. In principle, economic planners could then calculate the optimal allocation of resources for the leader. The leader would have his subordinates impose this allocation. Since conditions and technologies are constantly changing, optimality requires that the whole process continually be redone.

As has long been known, a bureaucracy cannot obtain or process all of the information needed to calculate an optimal allocation or put it into practice. Of course, given the amount of resources they mobilized through implicit taxation, the communist countries did not need optimality—they needed a minimal level of efficiency.

Obtaining the Information Needed for a Coherent Plan

For a Soviet-type economy to obtain a tolerable allocation—indeed, for it to function at all—the bureaucracy must centralize and exploit a staggering amount of information. In a market economy, only the firm needs to know how much output it can obtain from each combination of inputs. If each firm had this information about its production function and knew the prices of its outputs and inputs, then a market economy, if it were perfectly competitive, would generate an optimal allocation of resources. In a Soviet-type economy, by contrast, the central planners need (in addition to a lot of explicit and implicit markets) to know the production function of every enterprise. In order to work out an efficient plan, they need to use this information, as well as a very detailed knowledge of the leader's priorities.

The information obtained from the monitoring of performance and the experience of actual conditions becomes evident only at the front line of the production processes. This information has to be passed through layers of bureaucracy to the top. The orders worked out in the light of this information also have to pass through all of these layers of officials on the way down. When, as in agriculture and retail distribution, the economic activity takes place over large amounts of space, the transmission of information and the monitoring of activities is made more difficult by the distances involved. The information losses also increase disproportionately with the size of a bureaucracy, since mis- understandings at each layer of the hierarchy are normally passed on to all successive layers.

As Gordon Tullock, Oliver Williamson, and others have explained, the information problem in the large bureaucracy resembles the children's game of telephone where a message is whispered from one child to another and becomes increasingly distorted by each child who repeats it to the next person in line. In a large bureaucracy, there is inevitably a significant loss and distortion of information, even with the best efforts of all concerned.

For fundamental reasons, best efforts are not usually available. A manager's chances of promotion or bonuses are lowered if a superior learns of mistakes. Subordinates, therefore, have an incentive to hide performance shortcomings. There is also an incentive to overstate the difficulties faced and to understate potential production. The incentives to distort information accumulate at every level of a hierarchy, so they increase nonlinearly with the size of the bureaucracy and are bound to be exceptionally serious in a centrally planned economy. The more one reflects about these problems, the clearer it becomes that there must be a countervailing factor, or the centrally planned economies would not have been able to function at all.

Bureaucratic Competition

Competition among bureaucrats or between officials and workers is such a countervailing factor. The strong incentive for production facing the leader of a Soviet-type society can at times be translated into actual performance because of the constraints on bureaucratic misrepresentation and negligence. Each bureaucrat can be constrained by others in the same chain or series of productive activities—that is, by those who manage activities that either use the output of the activity managed by a given manager or supply an input for this activity. I shall call those managers and workers in the same productive sequence *serial* bureaucrats. Each bureaucrat can also be monitored by *parallel* managers and workers: those who, in a market economy, would be competitors.

Let us consider serial relationships first. Each subordinate is better off if his superior thinks he has, as it were, made lots of superb bricks with a little poor straw. A superior cannot observe the outputs and inputs of several subordinates as closely as each subordinate can observe his own output, and the superior's superior has even less opportunity for observation. So a subordinate can often make his performance look better than it really is.

This information problem is reduced somewhat because the managers of activities that are in series with a given manager's activity are well placed to make pertinent observations that the supervisory hierarchy often will not be able to make. The managers in series with a given manager also have incentives that countervail those of the manager in question. The manager of a construction project should know if the bricks were too few, too poor, or too late, and he normally has an incentive to report (if not exaggerate) such deficiencies. If the brick-making manager wrongly claims that he did not receive the needed straw, the supplier of the straw obviously also has corrective information and an incentive to provide it to superiors.

There is a chilling example of the information gains to the leadership from subordinates in a serial relationship in *The Inner Circle*, a book and a movie that are reportedly based on the real life of Stalin's film projectionist. A movie projector breaks down when Stalin is watching a film. Upon inquiring why, Stalin learns from the film projectionist that the Soviet-made film projector, though in other respects like the German-made projector on which it was modeled, fails because of an inadequate spring. Stalin points to the need to reach the Soviet masses with films about Soviet achievements, and a responsible high-ranking official in charge of making items such as movie projectors is purged. The general point is that the information from bureaucrats in serial relationships about the performance of organizations managed by other bureaucrats must have significantly improved the information available to the leader of a Soviet-type society, and thus helps to explain why these societies were able to become as formidable as they were.[2]

Interestingly, the Soviet Union used an elaborate system of impartial arbitrators or judges partly to adjudicate disputes between enterprises about the quality and timeliness of goods and services that enterprises supplied to one another. The decisions and reports of these arbitrators must have helped the center obtain better information. In the Soviet Union between 1968 and 1980, Gosarbitrazh agencies considered an estimated 650,000 to 700,000 disputes annually.[3]

As the theory here predicts, the quality problems in Soviet-type societies were most notorious in consumer goods. Partly this is explained by the earlier argument that the leadership gained from shifting resources from production of consumption goods for the population to satisfying the purposes of the leadership: it takes fewer resources to produce low-quality goods. But some consumer goods produced in the Soviet countries were so poor that both the regime and the consumers would have been better off with better quality—they were sometimes unsalable.

Note that individual consumers, unlike the managers of the state-owned enterprises, were not well placed to reach and influence parts of the hierarchy above the manager of the enterprise responsible for the deficiency. A factory manager could reach higher-ranking officials and credibly argue that it was impossible to fulfill his factory's assignment unless the supplying enterprises provided tolerable inputs. The individual consumer did not have a comparable opportunity, and consumers were not organized to make collective complaints. Thus, managers of enterprises that were supposed to supply goods to consumers were in a better position to conceal shoddy quality than were managers of enterprises producing goods and services for other state-owned enterprises. Intriguingly, the Soviet military industrial complex even had a reputation for better quality production for consumer goods, which it sometimes produced for its own management and employees, than did the regular consumer sector.

Now let us consider parallel managers. Bureaucrats who manage enterprises or activities that, in a market economy, would be called competitive firms, can constrain misreporting by a given manager and can give him an incentive to be more productive. Suppose that a manager understates the output that can be produced with the inputs that are being allocated to him, or that he produces much less than he could produce. Parallel managers who are given similar inputs and responsibilities then have an opportunity to make a good impression by promising or actually producing better outcomes. Thus, when there is bureaucratic competition among parallel administrators, each official must accordingly be cautious in underreporting the potential productivity of the resources being allocated to him or in underproducing with the resources he is actually given. An astute superior can accordingly use competition among subordinates to exploit their more detailed knowledge and to draw out better estimates of potential production and increased productivity.[4]

So long as there is no question that bureaucrats are competing rather than colluding with one another, those at the top of a planned economy or hierarchy that produces ordinary private goods can even create a special kind of competitive market. The minister in charge of a given industry can, in effect, ask his subordinates to submit bids—promises on how much output they will obtain from given amounts of resources.[5] In essence, the requests for resources and output projections of subordinates create a kind of auction market. The official at the top can then allocate the available inputs to the ministry among the bidders in the way that would generate the most output. The subordinates can use the same strategy with their subordinates, and so on down the line, and many of the efficiency-enhancing characteristics of competitive markets can thus be replicated within a planned economy. Of course, there are problems judging the credibility of different bids and other complications, so these systems will work quite imperfectly.

Nonetheless, when a bureaucracy is producing marketable goods that may be counted and even sold, and there is no question that the subordinates are competing with one another, the competition among them creates a kind of market, and there are some efficiency gains. When governments are producing public goods, for example, defense, public health measures, and basic scientific research that cannot be measured well, if at all, it is not normally possible to compare the quantity of output that different administrators or offices produce, so even the kind of informal market that has just been described is unworkable. But it can make a contribution to efficiency when— as in a Soviet-type economy—much of the hierarchy is producing marketable goods that can be counted and sold: then competition among officials at any level creates an informal kind of auction market that brings some modicum of efficiency to the hierarchically organized production.

Covert Collusion

The foregoing argument assumed that collusion of subordinates does not limit bureaucratic competition or reduce the information or power available to the center. For the early period of a Soviet-type economy (or a period after a purge, or a cultural revolution such as the one Mao instigated, or another total shake-up of a society), this is a fairly realistic assumption. But, as we noted earlier in this book, in stable environments, collusion and other types of collective action increase over time.

This collusion is likely to emerge first among the nomenklatura and other high-ranking bureaucrats. Whether Soviet administrators are in a serial linkage or in a parallel connection, they will normally constitute a small group. The enterprises that supply the major inputs for a given state enterprise and the enterprises that are major users of its output are often small in number, so there are only a few managers in a serial linkage. The same holds true for the enterprises or activities in parallel connection—the number is usually similar to the number of firms in an oligopolistic industry in a market economy. Indeed, the communist preference for unusually large plants and enterprises sometimes makes for even fewer managers in a parallel connection. (The numbers of workers doing "competitive" work and thus in parallel connection in a given state enterprise were, however, sometimes considerably larger.)

Because the numbers involved in most linkages, whether serial or parallel, are small, the managers can organize in much less time than would be required for large groups. However, the restraints on independent organization in a communist society—especially an organization that weakens the control of the leader—mean that collusion must be inconspicuous, informal, and secretive. Only after a considerable period of covert collusion, when a group has acquired such substantial insider influence that it is a political force in its own right, can a combination become explicit. The need to proceed covertly makes collective action emerge much more slowly than it otherwise would. Obviously, a really large number of people cannot organize secretly, so large groups (for example, independent trade unions) that would have weakened the control of the leadership did not emerge in communist countries.

Thus, as time goes on in a Soviet-type society, there are opportunities for many groups—especially small groups of high-

ranking administrators and enterprise managers in particular industries—to organize informally and covertly. As more time
passes, subordinates of subordinates organize. In time this small-
group covert collusion can reach down to coteries of senior
workers in factories, mines, collective farms, and retail shops.
Ultimately, even enterprises and industry associations can become combinations or insider lobbies that serve the interests of
their managers and members more than they serve the center or
the society. By this stage, so much power has devolved that combinations can sometimes use their power more or less openly.
How can administrators in a Soviet-type society gain from
covert collective action? And who loses from their collusion?

Collusion in Serial Linkages

With respect to managers in serial linkage, the gains from collusion were, at least for quite a long time, not especially large.
The leadership observed whether it was obtaining the final
outcomes it wanted. Though the subordinates responsible for
these outcomes had an incentive to blame suppliers for deficiencies, they were limited in their capacity to do this by the
interests of the suppliers, subsuppliers, and so on. Thus, especially in the military industrial complex, the leadership must
have continually reaped some gains from the information of
subordinates in serial relationships.

Nonetheless, at least where final outcomes were less likely
to be observed by the leadership (as with consumer goods for
the masses), covert cooperation among administrators made
things worse. Though the retail enterprises and health care
providers that served ordinary consumers, for example, could
immediately reap gains because they were rarely observed,
their suppliers could share in these gains only through collusion with those in the badly observed sector. When it could be

covertly worked out, retail enterprises and their suppliers could gain from supplying fewer goods to consumers and from keeping the savings for themselves. Ultimately, some interests in consumer retail sectors even worked against increased supplies of consumer goods, because with fixed prices, a smaller supply meant that the favors or even bribes that retail employees could receive for distributing the goods would be larger. In these cases, there was obviously scope for mutually advantageous collusion with suppliers.

With time, those in serial relationships, even in priority areas for the leadership, could also gain by colluding in various forms of misappropriation, even though it was the powerful "owner" of the society—the dictator or Politburo members—who lost from this misappropriation. In general, only the producing and receiving enterprises know exactly how much one supplies to the other. If their managers collude to skim off a little for themselves, this will be almost impossible for the leadership to observe, so all that is needed is reliable collusion among the parties. To the extent that high-ranking subordinates of the relevant managers can ultimately discern what is happening, the collective action can be expanded: more can be skimmed off and shared with them. The more commonplace such forms of collective action are, the less dangerous they become, and the wider the number who participate. Finally, this collusion becomes a norm, whole enterprises participate, and the fruits of such misappropriative collective action are needed to attract employees into an industry.[6]

Collusion in Parallel Linkages

It is with administrators in parallel linkage that discreet collective action really scores in Soviet-type societies. Consider an advance in knowledge that can increase the productive potential of a whole industry. If the leader of the country knows how much extra production could be obtained because of such an advance, then quotas could be increased accordingly and resources reallocated in order to reap the maximum gain. But the society and central planners cannot have full knowledge of the technological improvements available in each period to every industry. They are dependent on experts and managers in the industry itself. It is in the collective interest of the managers of enterprises in the industry, and of the manager of the industry as a whole, that the productive potential of these advances should be underestimated by the central leadership.

So long as the extra production that the industry leaders and enterprise managers are required to obtain from additional resources is not in fact the maximum obtainable (and only they, if anyone, know this maximum), then it will also be in their collective interest to receive more resources, because these resources can also be used in part to secure their personal objectives—to supplement the income or the leisure of management or the workers of enterprises. Thus, when collusion becomes commonplace, the managers of the establishments in an industry, whether separately or in league with the leader of the industry, have an incentive collectively to monopolize the information on the extra output obtainable from allocated resources in order to collude against those still higher up.

Collusion Eliminates Competitive Bidding

The informal market through which subordinates make promises or bids to their superiors in competition for resources loses its efficiency-enhancing qualities. If the subordinates at a given level in a given industry can engage in collective action, even covertly, they will gain from using this collective power to agree not to outbid one another. They can all agree to promise less and to deliver less in return for the resources they are allocated. Then there is a surplus that they can control and use in part for their own welfare.

Evidence of Collusion:
The Soft Budget Constraint

Ultimately, the devolution reaches the point where the income of an enterprise is not given by its contribution to the achievement of the Politburo's objectives or by the revenue from its sales but by its political administrative power. This outcome is most starkly evident in untypical cases, such as in Hungary for a time, where official recognition was given to the idea of a socialist price system that was supposed to copy and improve upon capitalist markets. Under this theory, the resources available to a state enterprise should be limited to its receipts and (with borrowing and equity finance) expected future receipts, as is true of private firms in a market economy: when prices are right, the operations of enterprises whose receipts do not cover their costs subtract from the total output of the economy.

What often happened, as the Hungarian economist Janos Kornai has pointed out, was that the resources available to a firm bore little or no relation to either its present or its prospective receipts. Firms with losses were about as likely to obtain resources as firms with profits. An indispensable requirement of a rational economy—that enterprises and activities that do not cover their costs will ultimately have to stop using up resources that subtract from society's income—was lost. Kornai called this absurd situation a "soft budget constraint," and this phrase fits perceptions of the late stages of communism so well that it has become famous in the economic literature. A soft budget constraint also implies, of course, that activities that earn a large surplus are not expanded as social rationality would require.

To see how the ultimate emergence of the soft budget constraint follows from the argument in this chapter, and to picture how catastrophic it has to be for economic performance, make the simple assumption that the political administrative power of an enterprise is proportional to its scale of operations or, alternatively, to the number of its employees. Then the total revenues of the relevant sector (the industry or ministry)— or (worse) of the whole economy—will be divided among the enterprises in proportion to their scale or their employment. There then will be no connection between the value of an activity or an enterprise and the amount of resources it receives! The devolution of political power in reality would not actually be in exact proportion to scale or employment, but it is likely to gravitate toward such proportions. Thus, the devolution that has been described ultimately robs the plans of a Soviet-type economy of even a modicum of rationality, either from the point of view of the autocrat or of the population. When the sclerotic process proceeds very far, the losses to society through the soft budget constraints are bound to be gargantuan.

Experts on Soviet-type societies have found many types of behavior that must also have been due to covert collective action. Jerry Hough and Merle Fainsod, for example, came to wonder "whether the familiar pattern of the regulated coming to dominate the regulators has not developed in the Soviet Union as well as the West."[7] Similarly, Michael Montias[8] describes a comparable process that took place in Polish society—a process that was largely instrumental in producing the Polish economic collapse of the late 1970s:

> The "ministerial lobbies," as they are now called, successfully pressed for more investments and more imports for the enterprises under their direction long after it had become obvious that increases in either would have nefarious consequences for the economy.

Again, in Hungary, both Andras Nagy[9] and Erzsebet Szalai[10] describe a process by which the collective action of large enterprises became a dominant and detrimental force in the setting of policy and in economic performance.

The foregoing accumulation of covert collective action would not be so damaging to the productivity of a Soviet-type society if each of the separate collusions, enterprises, and industry associations had a significant incentive to make the society work. But whereas the dictator or Politburo at the center has an encompassing interest in the productivity of the society, the separate collusions and special-interest organizations do not. Their incentives are quite as perverse as those of narrowly organized special interests in market democracies, and nearly as perverse as those of the individual criminal.

Law Enforcement and Corruption

Chapter 6 discusses the way in which market-contrary policies undermine law-abiding behavior and promote official corruption, because they create situations in which all of the parties involved have a common interest in evading the rules, keeping the evasion secret from the authorities, and corrupting the relevant officials. We know that the uniquely high rates of implicit tax collections in the Soviet-type systems implied great interference with markets and that this encouraged corruption under communism. But this market-contrary character of the Soviet-type systems does not adequately convey communism's corruption-inducing tendencies. This can best be understood by going back to our stationary bandit metaphor.

The most remarkable corruption-inducing feature of the Soviet-type systems becomes evident when comparing this system of implicit tax collection with the traditional types of autocratic tax theft. The autocrat who leaves the productive assets and production of the society in the hands of his subjects has to fight tax evasion, but much of the work of maintaining order is done by his subjects. Each subject tends to protect his property, which makes it possible for a traditional autocrat to keep theft among his subjects within bounds and also limits the exposure of his officials to bribery.

If, by contrast, an autocrat takes 100 percent of the rents, profit, and interest earned by the natural resources and tangible capital of his domain, and also sets the wages of workers in order to maximize the implicit tax on labor, then there is almost no private property or privately managed production. There is, apart from some personal items, almost no property that subjects guard in their own self-interest. Both the fixed assets and the inventory of every significant enterprise belong to the autocrat and he is the only person who has an automatic incentive to guard this property. In order to maximize implicit tax collections, almost all production has to be under the control of the autocrat and his subordinates, and so every manager is in part a tax collector.

The autocrat then has more property and more tax collection than any man can watch, so there must be watchers and also those who watch the watchers. If those who watch best and collect the most for the center are rewarded, and those who lose property and collect least are punished, then competition among the watchers and the collectors means that everyone is watched and all the collections are passed on: the watchers and collectors watch and collect from each other. Though they all would gain from overthrowing the stationary bandit and keeping his exactions for themselves, this overthrow would be a collective good for millions and no individual has an incentive to bear the costly risks of steps he or she would take toward obtaining this collective good.

Banding Together Against the Bandit

But within small groups, the autocrat's subjects can, when they eventually develop sufficient trust in one another, safely conspire together in their common interest. It is in their common interest to skim off part of the bandit's take. Whenever diversion of production, theft of state property, or failure to work conscientiously is observed only within the small conspiring group, it will not be detected by the center. Whatever the autocrat cannot observe with his own eyes, he can learn about only through reports of those beneath him. Each individual in a small group will obtain a significant share of the yield of collusion. As time goes on, more and more small groups explicitly or tacitly agree that they will do less work, allocate more of the resources under their control to their own purposes, and share more of the state property among themselves.

There are, however, limits to what a small group can take without being observed by someone outside the group. If the managers take too much, their subordinates may notice. If those in Department A take too much, those in Department B may know. So, if there is time for the manager and his subordinates, or Department A and Department B, to reach the point where they can trust each other with secrets, they can agree that more of the goods they produce and the assets they control will be kept for themselves. Eventually the enterprise, the industry, the locality, and even the ethnic or linguistic group come to agree, tacitly if not explicitly, that they can and should keep more for themselves: more and more of the central bandit's theft is taken back.

The center has those who watch the watchers: the higher officials, party cadre, police, secret police, and other watchdogs whose job is to ensure that none of the autocrat's property is stolen and that every enterprise, industry, locality, and ethnolinguistic group produces huge implicit tax collections for the center. But if no one except the center owns property, and if no one except the center has the legal right to claim the implicit tax receipts, then everyone except the center has an incentive to induce these officials to become a part of the countless conspiracies to take back some of what the stationary bandit has stolen from them.

If the watchdog officials can persuade the center that they are doing a great job guarding the property and increasing the implicit tax collections, they are likely to be rewarded. Even a small share of the gains from a diversion of production or the theft of assets is, however, likely to be worth more than the extra salary that comes from a promotion. The best outcome of all for the official is to be promoted and then take a share of the implicit tax collections and state property over a wider part of the economy. Of course, the center has an interest in preventing this, but it has virtually no source of information on what is happening other than subordinate officials, all of whom have an interest in being part of conspiracies and combinations that skim off as much as possible of the autocrat's take. If the harshest punishments are imposed on even the faintest suspicion, then the bureaucratic competition that is indispensable to the system can be preserved somewhat longer, so Stalinist purges are not so harmful to the system as has been supposed and might even make the system work better. In the long run, nonetheless, the difficulties of covert collective action are bound to be overcome in more and more enterprises, industries, localities, and ethnic or linguistic groups.

It is a law of motion of Soviet-type societies that they must not only run down over time but also become increasingly corrupt.[11] Ultimately, it becomes, some say, impossible to buy and easy to steal. More and more victims of the regime come to believe that he who refrains from taking state property is robbing his family. That is, part of the population comes to have a visceral, intuitive sense that it is only right that they should take something back.

Narrow Interests Replace the Encompassing Interest

The stationary bandit who takes everything except the minimum needed to elicit the effort of his captives has an encompassing interest in the productivity of the society, so he does what is necessary to make the society productive and better able to meet his needs. By contrast, each of the conspiring coteries, enterprise lobbies, industry associations, and local societies obtains so little of the society's output that each of them has only a narrow interest—that is, little or no incentive to maintain the productivity of the society. As communism devolved, it was bound to collapse.

When the argument in this chapter is taken in conjunction with the theory in prior chapters, it has a number of additional implications, especially for the societies in transition.

These implications are different from those that arise from conventional views of communism and of the transition. Thus, we can compare the predictions of the present argument—and the implications of familiar views—with the facts, which is the task of Chapter 9.

9

IMPLICATIONS FOR
THE TRANSITION

AT LEAST AT THE BEGINNING of the transition process, both those who preferred rapid shock therapy and those who preferred a gradual transition to a market economy tended to speak of the transition in the same terms: it was a change from a system governed by Marxist-Leninist ideology to one governed by capitalist-democratic ideas. Both sides still agree that the old system was predicated on the belief in state ownership and economic planning guided by the Communist party; by contrast, the system the societies in transition are establishing is predicated (as Western societies are) on the belief in private ownership and free markets with a democratic government. Now that communism has collapsed, it is taken for granted that the transition consists mainly in replacing state ownership and planning with private ownership and management: the essence of the transition is privatization of state-owned industry.

The most contentious question has been how fast the shift from state ownership and management to private ownership and management should occur. The shock therapists want rapid wholesale privatization and the gradualists want a slower governmentally planned and sequenced (and, in some cases, only partial) privatization. The debate is a battle of metaphors. The shock therapists say that you cannot jump a chasm in two leaps; the gradualists say that you do not ask a patient who has just had pneumonia to go out in the cold winds of competition to run a marathon.

There have been many intellectual and political disagreements about who should be (or should have been) the new private owners of the state-owned property and how the receipts from sales of state property should be shared. There has been a lot of concern that neither foreign corporations nor high-ranking managers and administrators from the old regime should obtain the valuable capital in the huge state enterprises at unfairly low prices (or for no price at all), and that the vast amount of capital that has been accumulated because of the high savings rates in the communist countries should be fairly shared.

This concern about ownership and receivership is important to the discussions among Western experts as well as to the political divisions in the societies in transition. Some Western economists, for example, argue (or once argued) that giving the state enterprises to their employees would be unfair, partly because workers in capital-intensive industries would arbitrarily receive more wealth than workers in labor-intensive industries; other economists have devised various schemes for mass privatization. It is well known that the Soviet-type regimes had exceptionally high rates of investment and accumulated huge quantities of capital, so it is (or once was) normally taken for granted that huge sums are at stake. In Germany, for example, the Truehandanstalt was created not only to manage and sell or operate the accumulated capital of the German Democratic Republic but also to hold the receipts from the sale and management of these assets in trust for the East German people.

Thus, the transition is seen by shock therapists and gradualists alike as a system governed by one ideology being replaced by a system governed by different ideas, and the privatization of state-owned enterprises is regarded as the essence of the process. The main question under dispute is how fast the existing state enterprises should be changed from state management to private management through privatization. There is obviously some truth in this conventional conception, and the question of how fast privatization should occur is clearly significant. Yet it is also troubling that this debate is conducted in substantial part through metaphors that cannot possibly guide the detailed choices that have to be made. The familiar views should also leave us puzzled about some of the most important things that are going on in the societies in transition.

The Puzzle of Rampant Inflation

In the very last years of communism and especially during the transition there has been rampant inflation. Neither Marxist-Leninist ideology nor liberal-democratic ideology advocate (or even condone) high rates of inflation. There is no economic theory that suggests either rapid or slow privatization can cause inflation. Whether enterprises are under private or public control, high rates of inflation are a major problem. So why have most of the transitions and sometimes the years immediately preceding them (e.g., Gorbachev's reign) been marked by rapid inflation? Neither the familiar view of the transition nor the major dispute about how it should be handled lead us to expect the rapid inflation that is occurring in many post-communist countries.

All schools of macroeconomic thought agree that when there is a government budget deficit that amounts to a substantial fraction of a country's gross domestic product—and this budget deficit is financed by creation of new money—

there will be inflation. Most of the societies in transition, all observers agree, have large government budget deficits that are financed by money creation. Neither the old nor the new ideologies justify these deficits nor lead people to expect them. Neither privatization nor its absence can explain these deficits. So why do so many of the societies in transition bring the curse of inflation upon themselves through huge monetized budget deficits?

The Decay and Collapse of a System of Taxation

Huge budget deficits are exactly what would be expected from the sclerotic erosion of a system of taxation. We saw that the Soviet-type societies had very little in the way of income taxes or other explicit taxes on individuals. Instead they had uniquely high rates of implicit taxation that they obtained by setting wages and prices at levels that would generate large profits in state-owned industrial enterprises. The autocrat claimed these profits.

As time went on, the combinations of managers, bureaucrats, and even workers covertly came to share control (and finally often to have the main control) over the state enterprises that were the principal source of tax receipts. These tax receipts diminished over time. What had been revenue for the center became costs—it was kept by the enterprise and its management, workers, and suppliers, or simply dissipated through inefficiency, or sometimes even literally stolen. As the center became poorer and weaker, it even had to worry about public opinion, which made it harder to restrict consumption, pensions, and social services even in hard times.

In the later years of communism, many of the Soviet-type countries found it necessary to borrow abroad, but the capacity to repay was so limited that some of these countries soon reached the limit of their capacity to borrow or even defaulted on their loans. By Gorbachev's time, the center was simply unable to pay its bills without printing a lot of new money, and in the very last days of the Soviet Union virtually no resources at all were passed on to the Soviet government. The regimes that in Stalin's time took uniquely large percentages of the national output for the state had by the end devolved to such an extent that they could not finance the basic services of government. The single most important source of the collapse of communism, I believe, was that the communist governments were broke.

With the collapse of communism and democratization, the center lost even more of its power. With democracy, the managements and workers in the large state enterprise were the main groups organized for collective action, and they no longer had to operate covertly. The most powerful lobbies and cartels in the new societies naturally were not about to act as tax collectors for the new center. On the contrary, they wanted—and received—subsidies. So the main source of tax revenues was lost and replaced by powerful new claimants for subsidies. Given the death of the tax system, the subsidies had to come mainly from new money issued by the banking system. The result was, as it had to be, even higher rates of inflation in most of the formerly communist countries.

No Large-Scale Privatization, Unless the Insiders Get It

If private management and market incentives make enterprises much more productive than state management and economic planning, then those who are managers or workers in a state enterprise (and thus have a claim on the revenues of that enterprise) should regularly want prompt privatization of the enterprise: if the enterprise becomes more productive, there should normally be a larger surplus from which they can obtain rewards for themselves. In some large state-owned enterprises, the management and workers do indeed want rapid privatization.

But in many large state-owned enterprises, there is a surprising and often intense opposition to privatization and economic reform generally. More often than not, if any mass privatization takes place, it is only privatization (such as that in Russia) that gives the firms mainly to the insiders and (especially) the existing management, and leaves the same managers in power as before. Though the commonplace assertion in many formerly communist countries that, with privatization of large-scale enterprise, nothing changes, is an exaggeration, it captures a fundamental reality: by the end of the communist period, the large enterprises were in large part too powerful politically to be controlled much by the center, and more often than not they have remained so powerful that, even if there is privatization, it is privatization in which almost nothing changes, unless it is change that the enterprise management itself wants.

In Russia, for example, many large state-owned enterprises had combined their lobbying powers in the Civic Union, which mainly opposed economic reform. When mass privatization did occur, it was only on a basis that gave most of the ownership of the privatized enterprises to their existing managements and workers. Throughout the formerly communist world, those who are employed by large state-owned enterprises are normally the most conservative. This opposition to privatization is often explained on ideological grounds and ideology presumably does have something to do with it. Yet we must be puzzled: if private management and market incentives would make those associated with a large state enterprise better off, why do they lead the opposition to it?

In many cases, truly market-oriented economic reforms will not, in fact, make those associated with large state-owned enterprises better off, at least not over any time span short enough for them to have confidence. When we think back to the sclerotic process described in Chapter 8, we immediately see why. Though there was (mainly because of the encompassing interest of the autocrat) some productivity-boosting basis for most investments in the early Stalinist phase of the Soviet-type societies, this was not true of the sclerotic years that immediately preceded communism's collapse. In this senile phase the organization of production and the allocation of investment depended as much on the insider political bureaucratic power of different enterprises and coteries for collective action as on relative productivities. With the soft budget constraint that the sclerosis brings, investment could not have been directed to its most productive uses.

The Carcass of Communism

Even the scope of activities within an enterprise and its scale became grossly irrational. In Poland, for example, the largest pig farm in the country was part of a state-owned steel-producing enterprise, and throughout the communist world enterprises combined activities that were rarely if ever combined in the market economies. Enterprises and plants in Soviet-type societies were also systematically much larger than most of those that survive the market test in the

Western economies. The main reason was that, with many prices and wages and the allocation of major inputs set by the regime, the enterprises could not count on buying what they needed. Thus, a steel plant might set up a pig farm to provide meat for its workers or a construction firm to make housing for its management and workers. The large state enterprises in the declining years of the Soviet-type societies usually did not have either the appropriate scope of products or the efficient scale: the very conception of most enterprises and the division of labor among them was fundamentally wrong.

The investments in most of these enterprises usually embodied obsolete technologies and were usually misdirected as well. In the most prosperous market economies, most machinery is replaced or sidelined in less than five years, so much of the investment made before 1989 or 1991 in the Soviet-type countries would be uneconomic even if it had been perfectly targeted and of the latest Western manufacture. When investments embody out-of-date technologies and are allocated according to socially irrational mechanisms, their value, especially after a couple of years, is often determined by the demand for scrap iron. Thus, much of the investment in the Soviet-type economies is now valueless.

The startling magnitude of the irrationality of the late allocation of resources is evident from a well-known study of East Germany by George Akerlof and others. Using a unique data source from which they could determine not only the value of diverse products exported by East German conglomerates but also calculate the value, in Western currency, of the inputs used to produce these exports, they found that only 8 percent of the East German workers were producing goods whose value in international markets covered even the variable costs of producing these products.[1] If only one worker in twelve was engaged in viable and socially efficient production in East Germany, one of the most prosperous of the communist economies, then it is unlikely that things were much better in other Soviet-type economies.

Thus, a rational allocation of current resources would have very little in common with the allocation on the eve of communism's collapse. The development economist Anne Krueger has estimated that 80 to 90 percent of South Korea's productive factors in the 1970s were used for something different from what they had been used for in 1960.[2] The replacement of communism with a market economy is comparable to the change that South Korea underwent from an underdeveloped to a newly industrializing country.

Even the organization of labor and work habits in the typical mature Soviet-type enterprise were uneconomic. Many multinational firms and new firms operating in the societies in transition refuse to hire locals who have experience in their industry! I once read an account in the *Washington Post* of an Austrian hotel chain operating in the former Soviet Union that refused to hire local workers who had experience in the Soviet hotel industry. Thinking that this story was, while probably unique, most instructive, I passed it on to others, only to hear of comparable policies in other Western hotel chains in the former Soviet Union. Then I quickly came upon reports of a Polish businesswoman with a successful set of women's clothing stores who refuses to hire anyone who has worked in the Polish state fashion industry, and an entrepreneur who created a successful Russian private airline and refuses to hire anyone who has worked for Aeroflot for his cabin crews.[3]

There is a reason why the managements and workers of many large state enterprises do not want privatization or other economic reforms: Soviet-style sclerosis has gone so far that their enterprises often could not be viable in a competitive marketplace and would not be maintained in a rational economy.

Misconceptions in Debates About Privatization

Just as Stalinism was not so much an ideology about what type of economic organization will serve society best as it was a system of implicit tax collection, so the debate about the speed of privatization also focuses more on the surface than on the deeper reality. The more fundamental issue is not whether certain assets should be under public or private management—most of the opponents of reform in state-owned enterprises would probably be delighted to work in profitable private enterprises, and some of them have made precisely that shift.

The deeper issue arises out of the conflict of interest between those in socially productive new enterprises and those whom the accidents of history have left in many state enterprises that can live only through subsidies from the rest of society. It is the subsidy, not the private or public status, that matters most, both for economic efficiency and for the interests of subsidy recipients. In many (if not most) cases, it is not the speed of privatization that matters but the speed of liquidation.

There may well be an indirect link between privatization and liquidation: subsidies probably are less conspicuous in a planned economy than in a market economy, and private owners would not continue an activity that brought only losses unless they received subsidies. Yet a rational planned economy, like an open competitive market, would not continue many of the state enterprises sustained in the sclerotic last years of communism, so the issue of private versus public management is not the essence of the matter. At the very core there is the conflict between parasitic and productive sectors.

The Internal Contradictions

Unfortunately for the societies in transition, it is mainly the large state-owned (or lately privatized) enterprises, many of which are uneconomic, that are organized for collective action. Whereas the defeated totalitarian countries in World War II were left largely free of organizations for collective action, the countries that were under communist control have been left with an incomparably more severe form of the British disease. They have been bequeathed a substantial number of governmentally established and often still publicly funded insider lobbies. These lobbies are the large state enterprises (the small ones usually do not have lobbying or cartelistic power).

The serious problem arises from the percentage of these large state enterprises that are uneconomic under any management, private or public. The managers and workers in these state enterprises that will be competitive in an open market economy have no reason to resist privatization; though they will also make use of their power for collective action in their own interests, this power will not do much damage. The problem is the depressingly large percentage of organizations for collective action in the formerly communist countries that have interests that are inherently inconsistent with economic efficiency. Ironically, it was Karl Marx who coined the right phrase for this: there is, because of disproportionate power for collective action of the uneconomic enterprises, an "internal contradiction" in the societies in transition from communism to democracy.

The Exception That Proves the Rule

In spite of the many different types of evidence that support the foregoing argument, there may be some doubt that arises from the apparent lack of a test of the argument across different communist countries. In *The Rise and Decline of Nations* it was possible to compare the experience of many different countries (and even different states of the United States), all of which had market economies. Britain and the older northeastern parts of the United States had about the same system as West Germany, Japan, and the newer western and southern U.S. states, so the relationship between differences in the extent of narrowly based organizations for collective action and economic outcomes could be understood more easily. Was there a similar difference of experience among communist countries?

As it turns out, there was. We recall that small groups, especially at nomenklatura levels, could, in fullness of time, engage in covert collective action even in a communist dictatorship. Each of these small groups had a narrow interest that contrasted with the encompassing interest of the dictator. Thus, they had incentives to undermine economic efficiency and to resist market-oriented reforms that would increase competition. As Jan Winiecki has shown,[4] this resistance kept effective market-oriented reforms from being adopted in all of the Soviet-type economies in Europe. The nomenklatura coteries became better entrenched as time went on and they could block reforms that would expose their collusive gains to open competition.

One communist country went through a destruction of collusions for collective action that was equivalent to the organizational destruction in Germany and Japan. This was China during the cultural revolution. For whatever reasons, Mao started a revolution against his own upper-level and middle-level subordinates—the red mandarins. He decimated the very administrators and managers on which his economy depended. Only the military was spared. The immediate result was extreme instability and administrative chaos: the economic performance of the Chinese economy during the cultural revolution was much worse than in other communist countries. A longer-run result was that, when Mao died, there were not nearly as many well-entrenched coteries of administrators as in the Soviet Union and the European communist states.

So when Deng and the other pragmatists defeated Mao's widow and the rest of the "gang of four" shortly after Mao's death, there were few industries, enterprises, or coteries of administrators whose insider lobbying could undermine Deng's market-oriented reforms. Deng was presumably also helped because virtually everyone was glad to see the end of the chaos. The encompassing interest of Deng, the new pragmatic autocrat, prevailed, largely because the cultural revolution had destroyed the narrowly entrenched interests with a stake in the status quo.

Deng could do what Gorbachev and the other European communist reformers could not do: win out over the countless cliques engaged in covert collective action and other insider lobbies. The lion's share of the then-poor Chinese economy—agriculture—was promptly put under an individual responsibility market system. Other market-oriented reforms followed. The result, as we know, was rapid economic growth: output has often increased at 10 percent or more per year. This difference between China and the European countries that were communist, but had no cultural revolution, is precisely consistent with the argument offered here.

The Contrast Between Postfascism and Postcommunism

Compare the years immediately after Germany and Japan became independent democratic governments after World War II with the years since democratic or new governments replaced the communist regimes. Though I would not be surprised by impressive economic performance in the coming years by some formerly communist countries, it is already clear that the economic miracles are slow in coming. Whereas the peoples of West Germany and Japan were pleasantly surprised by their economic successes, the peoples of most of the postcommunist countries have to a great extent been disappointed with the fruits of freedom. The Soviet-type economies were so inefficient that it should be an easy matter to greatly outperform them, but some countries have found it difficult to even maintain the level of output they had under communism. Though it is no doubt a transitional problem, the peoples of the formerly communist countries are certainly within their rights to wonder why the transition is as painful as it is and why it takes so long.

The best insight into the contrast between the postfascist and the postcommunist experience may come from looking at their very different political experiences. There are tiny minorities in West Germany and Japan, composed substantially of cranks and skinheads, who advocate a return to the types of dictatorships that these countries had during World War II, and they attract a lot of publicity. But their utter marginality and the lack of respect that most of their fellow citizens have for them is dramatically revealed in the elections, when such groups, if able to get on the ballot at all, obtain practically no electoral support.

By contrast, in several countries that were under communist control, the former communist parties have obtained more votes in some elections than any other single party, and in some countries communist parties under one name or another have recaptured the government through free elections. Even though the thinking of these communist parties has changed significantly since the salad days of communism, this is still a remarkable development. The disappointment of the electorate in Russia, at least, is also evident in the remarkable degree of support for essentially fascist political leaders. Why has this happened, when Nazi or Tojo-type parties cannot win substantial support in West Germany or Japan?

As I see it, the single most important reason is that the West German and Japanese societies worked much better in the early years of their postwar democratic government than most of the formerly communist countries have worked in the years immediately after the collapse of communism. Naturally enough, the West Germans and the Japanese have not been anxious to go back to the kind of rule they had endured during World War II and the years that immediately preceded that war. For most of us, it is sad, but it should not be so surprising, that many people in the formerly communist countries find the new conditions unsatisfactory, even by the sorry standards of communist times.

Though part of the reason why things worked out better in the formerly Axis countries will be evident only after we have completed the next chapter, another part of the reason is evident now. Given the nature of the dictatorships that ruled Germany and Japan during World War II and the defeat and Allied occupation of those countries, they had very little in the way of narrow special-interest lobbying or cartelization in the early years of their postwar democracy. They were ruled mainly by majorities and therefore by relatively encompassing interests. Though these majorities made mistakes, their encompassing character gave them an incentive to try to make their societies work, and to a significant degree they succeeded.

By contrast, the sclerotic devolution of the system of extraction that Stalin had established left the formerly communist countries with large enterprises that were much
better at insider lobbying than at producing. Each of these
organizations has only a narrow stake in the prosperity of
society and has, in seeking to serve its interests, taken little
or no account of the needs of the society. These organizations have not only been a direct source of conservative and
sometimes procommunist argument but they have also—
through their lobbying and their demands for credits from
the central banks as well as through their failures to produce and trade efficiently—kept the formerly communist
countries from being nearly as productive as they could be.
This situation, in turn, has fostered the disappointment and
nostalgia that has brought support to conservative—and
sometimes even explicitly communist or fascist—political
parties.

What Remains to Be Done

Earlier in this book I examined autocracy, democracy,
Coaseian bargains, collective action, the sources of law enforcement and corruption, and postwar economic performance in the West. In this chapter and Chapters 7 and 8, I
focused on what the system that Stalin created really was, on
why it ran down over time, and on how the problem of the
transition away from communism is often misconceived. But
I have not yet dealt with how to make a market economy
thrive. There was no adequate theory of most of the matters
we have discussed so far, so developing that theory was the
first task. By contrast, there is a well-known theory of markets that has developed steadily over more than two cen-

turies, and there has been no need to explain that theory again here.

The standard theory of markets is missing an indispensable part: it is like an otherwise superb stool that has only two legs. The reason that the third leg of the theoretical stool is missing, I believe, is that the discipline of economics emerged and developed mostly in the relatively successful economics. It began in the same time and place as the Industrial Revolution—Adam Smith's *The Wealth of Nations* was published in Great Britain in 1776 and almost all of the advances in the subject have taken place in the highly developed economies of Western Europe and North America. All of the societies in which economic theory developed had a common feature that was normally taken for granted (and, if thought of at all, regarded as matter for other disciplines). The legs of supply and demand, as it were, could appear to hold up the stool by themselves because am indispensable third prop for the theory was so commonplace it was not even noticed. The prop was there in the societies about which the economists wrote, but not in the theory or the textbooks.

This did not matter so much as long as economists attempted to explain only the types of societies in which the subject emerged. But when economics has turned its attention to the societies of the third world or the second-world societies in transition from communism, the missing theoretical leg leaves the analysis without balance. When the student in the second or third world reads even the finest abstract work on economic theory, he or she is given the impression that this work is so general that it must hold even on other planets. Yet these works do not tell the students of the second or third worlds why they read a book surrounded by poverty, or why it was written in an environment of wealth. It is to this question that we now turn.

10

THE KINDS OF MARKETS
NEEDED FOR PROSPERITY

THOUGH MANY PEOPLE EMPHASIZE that all of the successful economies use markets extensively, I have rarely heard anyone point out that markets are ubiquitous in the poor economies as well. This is evident even from the most casual observation. Those who live in low-income economies know that there are shops and market days in the villages, bazaars in the towns, and peddlers hawking their wares on the street. The number of shops and peddlers in a large, poor city such as Calcutta is almost uncountable. The largest number of markets that I have ever seen in one place was in far-from-prosperous Moscow in early 1992, where there were people buying and selling at almost every metro stop and street corner.

There can be no doubt that all of the prosperous economies are market economies, and those who understand these economies know that the market is, at the least, a major source of their prosperity. As the Preface asked, if markets breed prosperity, why don't the ubiquitous markets in the low-income economies[1] make these economies prosperous too? Why, even though there are markets almost everywhere, are riches so rare? How can a society not only have markets but also the sort of market economy that generates vast wealth for its citizens?

These are crucial questions for the majority of the world's population living in the third world, where markets have long been ubiquitous. They are also important for the societies in transition from communism: most of their peoples are not satisfied with the abandonment of communism, but they also want the type of market economy that will generate incomes as high as those in the West. Indeed, these are key questions for people throughout the world, for no country, communist or capitalist, developing or developed, has the prosperity that it could have.

Different Kinds of Markets

Some people argue that the individual behavior required for markets occurs only in societies with an appropriate common culture. For example, an influential school of sociology that descends from Talcott Parsons contends that markets presuppose a prior consensus, often coming from a common religion, about basic values.

The argument here is that some types of markets regularly emerge whether or not the participants have anything in common, and sometimes even when participants have antipathy toward one another. These markets emerge spontaneously and some of them are literally irrepressible. I call them *self-enforcing* markets. By contrast, some other types of markets, which I call *socially contrived* markets, emerge only when a society maintains certain institutional arrangements. These special institutional arrangements are found on a continuing basis only in the richest countries of the world, but their profound importance is not understood even in these countries.

Spontaneous Markets

That many markets emerge spontaneously is evident even from the ancient world. Consider the following passage from Herodotus's *The History*:

> The Carthaginians also say that there is a place in Libya, and people living in it, beyond the Pillars of Heracles. When they, the Carthaginians, come there and disembark their cargo, they range it along the seashore and go back again to their boats and light a smoke signal. The natives, as soon as they see the smoke, come down to the shore and then deposit gold to pay for the merchandise and retreat again, away from the goods. The Carthaginians disembark and look; if they think the price deposited is fair for the merchandise, they take it up and go home again. If not, they go back to their boats and sit there. The natives approach and bring more gold in addition to what they have brought there already, until such time as the Carthaginians are persuaded to accept what is offered.

There was, of course, no common culture, court system, or government to facilitate trade between the Carthaginians and their partners, but it took place nonetheless. Indeed, it seems from Herodotus's account that this particular trade had even taken place often enough for signals to be recognized and certain procedures to have become customary. The parties probably expected to gain from similar trades in the future and thus found it in their interest to avoid anything that would prevent future trade.

There are many other examples from many different cultures of this "silent" trade, or transactions between individu-

als who have no government or institutions, and perhaps also
no religion or language, in common. There are, for example,
even accounts of tribes at war that have arranged trades with
each other through their women.[2] Some of the soldiers in the
Russian armies who fought the Chechen rebels also sold
Russian military equipment to these rebels. There has also
been a lot of trade in prisoner-of-war camps, with cigarettes,
for example, serving as a medium of exchange.

There are also gains from trade that cannot be realized by
the silent trade or in conditions such as those described by
Herodotus. The Carthaginians and the natives could not have
worked out a long-term loan, no matter how much one party
would have gained from borrowing even at high interest rates
and no matter how much the other would have liked a high
return on its capital. If one of the parties had wanted to buy
insurance against an adverse contingency, or to buy something made-to-order from the other, he would again probably
not have been able to work out the deal. The foregoing types
of transactions presumably could not have been realized because the parties had no court and legal system that would enforce the necessary contracts. This problem is best left aside
until we have dealt with the markets that are not only spontaneous but irrepressible.

Irrepressible Markets

The irrepressibility of some markets can best be illustrated
with the aid of a parable of two managers of state-owned enterprises in a totally planned economy. Suppose that the planners unknowingly give Enterprise 1 more of input A than it
needs. At the same time, they have unknowingly failed to allocate enough of input B to meet its production quota. The

planners happen to have given Enterprise 2 more of input B than it should have been given, but not enough of input A. Each of the enterprise managers will, of course, have an incentive to argue to higher authorities that he has not been given enough of the particular input his enterprise needs most, but he will also have an incentive to argue that his enterprise needs more of almost everything (i.e., that it needs what would, in a market economy, simply be a larger budget). Given that each enterprise manager normally has an incentive to say that his enterprise needs more inputs, neither can count on the planners accepting his argument, or on them being able to give him the needed input in time. Neither of the enterprise managers has an incentive to reveal to his superiors that he has been given a needlessly large allocation of an input.

In this case, each manager can sell the input that he has in surplus to the other, if he can do so without being observed by higher authorities, thereby solving both shortages. If the managers are discreet, this deal will normally make them better off, for each will have control over a more valuable bundle of inputs when he has traded his surplus input for another input that he badly needs. This type of trade will usually also make the planned economy work better, since the trade increases production by correcting a shortcoming in the design or implementation of the plan.

Trades of this type became so common in the Soviet Union that the Russian word *tolkach*, for pusher or expediter, was commonly used to refer to the person sent out to barter for scarce inputs and intermediate goods. Even though illicit trades undercut the ideology, rationale, and laws of a planned economy, they became so commonplace and indispensable that many of them were, in varying degrees, tacitly countenanced by many higher officials. Illegal or semilegal markets became so numerous and varied in the communist countries that it would not do to speak of all of these markets as "black" markets; one émigré expert on the Soviet economy found from his experience and research at least seven names or shades of gray were needed to distinguish the different degrees of official disapproval of different markets.[3] All of these various black, gray, and off-white markets are, in my classification, irrepressible. It is because so many markets are irrepressible that, as Chapter 6 argues, market-contrary policies always generate large shadow economies and lots of corruption in government.

As we know, the irrepressible markets, together with some of the smaller-scale spontaneous but not necessarily illegal markets, constitute the informal sector. This terminology is used most often in discussions of the third world. Though it is important to know that many markets are so irrepressible that they show up in great variety even in the communist societies that restrict markets the most, there is a still larger number of irrepressible markets in the third world (and also more than a few in the developed nations of the West).

The Informal Sector

The informal sector was first identified and explained by Keith Hart,[4] an economist working for the International Labor Organization. Many low-income people in third-world countries earn their livelihoods by peddling goods on the street; by repairing cars or equipment outside of registered garages; by providing diverse services to neighbors and friends; by selling urban transportation in old cars, vans, pickups, or buses that compete with the state-owned or public utility municipal transportation system that usually has a legal monopoly over such services; or by diverse other activities. In most cases, these commonplace activities are not fully legal. The individuals in the informal economy often lack the literacy needed to fill out the many forms needed to obtain permission to operate legally, or they do not have the money for (or do not want to pay) the bribes needed to obtain all of the required permits. Because many of these informal activities are small in scale and each minientrepreneur is usually inconspicuous, they often can avoid paying most taxes, which in third-world countries are usually sufficiently high as to make an activity uneconomic if it is fully taxed.

Much of the urban housing in many third-world cities is also informal. As the Peruvian writer Hernando DeSoto has vividly explained,[5] groups of low-income Peruvians (usually Indians who had recently migrated from a given traditional rural community) would coordinate a mass invasion, often in the dead of night, to unwatched or unused land in the outskirts of Lima, and immediately erect shanties to live in and picket-line defenses that reduced the likelihood the police would evict them. Much of the population of many cities in Latin America and other third-world countries live in such illicit or not-yet-legalized squatter settlements.

By their very nature, informal and illegal activities are hard to measure. Hernando DeSoto and his colleagues have estimated that a huge proportion of economic activity in Lima is informal. Whether their estimates are correct or not, there can be no doubt that informal activity is substantial in most third-world countries, and that it was also quite significant in the communist countries (and remains so in the transition). It is relatively lower in the developed democracies, but several studies suggest that it is not trivial and may be increasing.

Why Markets Exist Everywhere

The evidence of trade by primitive peoples, the parable of trade by discreet managers, and the large sizes of informal sectors in the second and third worlds show indisputably that many markets are spontaneous and are often irrepressible. Trade often takes place in the absence of a common culture or institutions to facilitate it and often in environments hostile to markets. When trade is not legal, the participants must add to the other costs of trade an allowance for the possibility that they will be apprehended and punished, and they also know that they cannot use the resources of the legal system to prevent misdeeds by another party or to enforce the terms of a contract.

We should not be surprised that a great deal of trade occurs even in inauspicious conditions. The gains from the division of labor and trade are, in the aggregate, so immense that most of the world's population could not survive without them. Some of these gains can be realized immediately in on-the-spot transactions. The markets that exist everywhere meet both of the following conditions: (1) the gains from making the trades are significant and (2) the trades are self-enforcing: each party to the transaction can largely eliminate the danger that the other will not reciprocate by making both parts of the transaction simultaneous, by making trades only within families or other close social groups where the aggrieved individual can bring social sanctions to bear, by restricting trades to those who have invested too much to obtain a reputation for honoring deals to profit from failing to do so, and so on. Thus some markets exist virtually everywhere, even when there is no legal system to enforce contracts and sometimes also when trade is illegal.

Does Misguided Interventionism
Make Markets Nearly Useless?

At this point, some people may, while conceding that markets are ubiquitous worldwide, object that the gains from these markets are largely eliminated by government intervention; the rampant and usually misguided government intervention in the third-world markets (to say nothing of the still-worse case of the communist economies) may make them nearly useless, thus explaining why most of the economies with ubiquitous markets remain poor. Though this objection obviously has some merit, it is—for a reason that has somehow normally escaped notice—mostly wrong.

Most of the gains from a market are usually realized even with prices or quantities that depart considerably from efficient levels. Suppose that the price of the water in a typical American town were set arbitrarily at $10 a liter, which is obviously a huge multiple of its usual marginal cost. Irrational as such a price would be, most of the gains from the consumption of water would still be obtained. Most people would no longer water their lawns or wash their cars, but almost all would buy enough water to maintain their health and quench their thirst: the water they would purchase would still yield most of the gains from trade in water.

More generally, suppose that a government arbitrarily sets a price at such an irrational level that only half as much is traded as would be traded in an ideal competitive market. Even in such a case, most of the total gains from trade will usually be realized, because the most valuable trades—the ones that generate the largest social surplus—will tend to occur. Since supply curves usually slope upward and demand

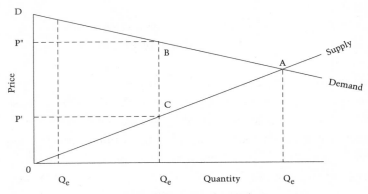

FIGURE 10.1   ◆   Less than Proportional Social Losses

curves always slope downward, an arbitrary price that pre-
vents half of the mutually advantageous trades from occurring
will not normally eliminate anything like half of the gains
from trade! This extremely simple point is demonstrated in a
footnote, which also shows that it is, of course, possible to fix
a price so far from equilibrium levels that it eliminates most
(or even all) trades and more than half (or all) of the gains from
trade; this will not happen very often unless the price-setters
are extraordinarily perverse.[6]

An arbitrary price imposes some extra costs from queuing,
retrading, or similar phenomena, and those losses are another
reason why arbitrary prices are undesirable. If the officially
fixed price is too low, there will be a waste of time waiting in
line, but the buyers with the most urgent needs will usually
be the first ones standing in the line or the ones who repur-
chase the good informally from those standing in line. The
suppliers who can produce the good most cheaply are the ones

who will have an incentive to produce and sell the good that is underpriced. If a good is overpriced, those who value it most highly will still obtain it, and the producers who have the lowest costs of production will have the greatest incentive to produce the amount that can be sold at the excessive price.[7] (An analogous argument holds for governmentally stipulated quantities.) It follows that, irrational as arbitrarily fixed prices are, markets with such prices will not reduce the gains from trade nearly so much as they reduce the quantity of trade.[8]

Socially Contrived Markets and Rights-Intensive Production

Harmful as those governmental interventions that introduce price distortions are for social efficiency, misguided government intervention in markets is by no means sufficient to explain why most countries with ubiquitous markets are poor. To understand this, we must also go beyond the types of trade and production that we have considered so far in this chapter: we must go beyond the self-enforcing or on-the-spot trades and beyond self-protected and labor-only (or very labor-intensive) production. We must also understand the gains from trade that are realized only in governmentally contrived or (more generally) socially contrived markets, and also the gains from individual rights–intensive production.

The Parable of the Self-Made Entrepreneur

A quick appreciation can be obtained of the social importance of trades that are not self-enforcing, and of the institutions that are needed to obtain the gains from certain kinds of trade and production, from another parable: that of the self-made entrepreneur. Suppose that a young man from a low-income family has no capital but a lot of ambition, energy, and entrepreneurial ability. In the same society there are individuals with wealth, but some of them do not happen to have as much productive ability as the self-made entrepreneur. There are also old people with accumulated savings but not so much energy. Since the poor young man can get more productivity out of capital than his rich and elderly counterparts, he can afford to pay them more out of the income he could generate with their assets than they can earn when they employ these assets themselves. There is, therefore, a potential for mutually advantageous trade under which some of the accumulated resources of the rich and of the elderly are lent to the self-made businessman or are invested as equity in a business he creates.

Suppose that the best use of the capital is for the able man to construct a factory that will last for thirty years. Such a transaction obviously makes no sense for the rich and the elderly unless they can be confident that the young man will not just keep the money for himself. The harvest of the investment is earned over thirty years and no one can know that the young man will honor his promises for that long. Given that the transaction in question is not by any means self-enforcing, the young man will have little chance to raise the capital needed for his productive enterprise, unless he can ensure that he will be required, on pain of having his assets seized, to keep his promise over the thirty years. If the capital in question is to be put under the control of the young man, he and the owners of the capital must agree on a contract that each believes is in his interest, expecting that this contract will be impartially enforced. Those with the capital may well insist that they hold a mortgage on the factory, or that a joint stock company be created in which they own most of the stock.

Potential lenders also may not participate unless they have a secure right to sell the asset they obtain as a result of the transaction in secondary markets, whether it be the asset of the young man's promise to repay or the corporate stock of the company he manages. Many elderly individuals without heirs, for example, would not rationally lend money for (or buy stock in) a project that finishes paying off only after they are dead unless they expect that they can advantageously sell the loan or the stock at an earlier time. Thus, all the institutions required for an ongoing and widely used capital market may be needed if some productive projects are to be financed.

The Needed Institutions

To realize all the gains from trade, then, there has to be a legal system and political order that enforces contracts, protects property rights, carries out mortgage agreements, provides for limited liability corporations, and facilitates a lasting and widely used capital market that makes the investments and loans more liquid than they would otherwise be. These arrangements must also be expected to last for some time.

Without such institutions, a society will not be able to reap the full benefits of a market in insurance, to produce complex goods efficiently that require the cooperation of many people over an extended period of time, or to achieve the gains from other multiparty or multiperiod arrangements. Without the right institutional environment, a country will be restricted to trades that are self-enforcing.

To realize the gains from complex transactions and those that take place over a long time, the individuals in a society not only need the freedom to trade but also the right to establish secure title to property and to mortgage property. They must have guaranteed access to impartial courts that will enforce the contracts they make, as well as the right to create new forms of extended cooperation and organization, such as the joint-stock corporation.

Analogous propositions hold for production as well as trade. Some types of production are more or less self-protected, such as food gathering, the making of handicrafts, personal services, and other mainly labor-only or labor-intensive types of production; these types of production may be advantageously undertaken even in environments in which there are no individual rights to property or to contract enforcement. But many other types of production require valuable assets, such as machines and factories or offices, that cannot be hidden and accordingly are exposed to seizure or confiscation. These types of production are property-rights intensive—the familiar expression capital intensive obscures the crucial role of enforceable rights. No one would normally engage in capital-intensive production if he or she did not have rights that kept the valuable capital from being taken by bandits, whether roving or stationary.

Many other important types of production are based almost entirely on contracts that are not self-enforcing. The production of the services that banks and related institutions provide can take place only when compliance with contracts is reliable: we would not deposit our money in banks (i.e., make the bank a loan that we can recall whenever we write a check or make a withdrawal) if we could not rely on the bank having to honor its contract with us, and the bank would not be able to make the profits it needs to stay in business if it could not enforce its loan contracts with borrowers. The production of insurance services or of hedges on futures markets is similarly uneconomic if contracts are not enforceable.

Individual Rights as a Cause of Prosperity

In short, in a market economy many important gains from trade and many important types of production will take place only if the individuals and firms have a broad and secure set of individual rights. In fact, gains from trade beyond those that primitive societies can obtain are often attainable only in environments where individual rights are both extensive and secure. Similarly, in at least market economies, those types of production that are not so elemental that they are self-protected can take place only if the rights to property and contract enforcement are secure.

Yet individual rights are often regarded as morally desirable but costly to economic performance—as a luxury that the less developed countries, or countries in especially difficult situations, may need to do without. We can now see that this view is, at least for market economies, utterly erroneous, and that we are back to the theory of dictatorship and democracy in Chapters 1 and 2. We can now see, for example, the immense importance of the short time horizons that must sooner or later come to a dictator.

We can also see why it is no accident that the developed democracies with the best established individual rights are also the societies with the most sophisticated and extended transactions (such as those in futures, insurance, and capital markets) for realizing the gains from trade. They are generally the societies with the highest levels of per-capita income.

Individual Rights and High-Powered Incentives

Individual rights are important to economic performance in other ways. We can see one of these other respects when we reflect on the inherent unpredictability of economic life. No one has the foresight needed to make the right decisions about where resources should be invested. As the old saying goes, prophecy is difficult, especially with respect to the future. In fact, it is worse than difficult: John Maynard Keynes exaggerated only a little when he said that "the inevitable never happens; it is the unexpected always." Some people are even worse at forecasting than others, often because they are not perceptive enough to know that they do not know the future and thereby fail to take into account as many possibilities as others do. As Rousseau said, it is essential to have "the ability to foresee that some things cannot be foreseen."

While some are worse at making prophecies than others, there is no one who can regularly make general and reliable forecasts. Yet every investment entails some explicit or implicit prediction. A modern economy is a wondrously complex system that continually converges toward a general equilibrium. But it always fails to reach equilibrium because it incessantly faces new opportunities and shocks. There is not even enough information to calculate the present situation of an economy with any detail or accuracy, much less its future position. The society as a whole is even more complex than the market economy and there are the uncertainties of international relations as well.

Because uncertainties are so pervasive and unfathomable, the most dynamic and prosperous societies are those that try many, many different things. They are societies with countless thousands of entrepreneurs who have relatively good access to credit and venture capital. There is no way that a society can predict the future, but if it has a wide enough span of entrepreneurs able to make a broad enough array of mutually advantageous transactions, including those for credit and venture capital, it can cover a lot of the options—more than any single person or agency could ever think of.

At least when a society has the appropriate institutions and government policies, the overwhelming majority of the firms that make huge profits are doing a huge service to the population. In a society with the right institutions and public policies, the prevailing prices will approximate the true values and costs of marginal quantities of the goods and productive inputs. A great excess of revenues over costs means that the enterprise is almost certainly putting more value into the society than it is taking out.

Many Fortunes Are Due to Luck

Since no one knows the future, a large part of the fortunes and losses in a modern economy are explained by luck as much as by the strengths or failings of the entrepreneurs involved. Some of those who correctly celebrate the social importance of the entrepreneur, and emphasize that it is impossible to get the information needed to design a rational plan for an economy, fail to point out that many entrepreneurs have been successful because they have been lucky. By the same token, many of the unsuccessful have been unfortunate.

In part because luck plays a large role, there is everywhere some tendency to treat very high rates of profit as unconscionable and to treat exceptional losses as social problems that a humane government should remedy. This thinking, in turn, often leads to subsidies to industries, enterprises, and localities that lose money. In the economies in transition, these subsidies are part of the soft budget constraints that are analyzed in an earlier chapter.

Social Insurance for Individuals Versus Groups

At the level of individuals, covering some of the losses of the unfortunate from the windfalls of the lucky makes moral sense. In the market democracies, the private insurance market and social insurance mechanisms of the modern welfare state redistribute income to the victims of bad luck. I have shown elsewhere that some transfers of consumption from those who have the most to those who have the least can increase the well-being or utility of the individuals in a society.[9]

The pertinent point here is that subsidizing industries, firms, and localities that lose money, even if it is due solely to bad luck, at the expense of those that make money, even as a result of pure chance, is typically disastrous for the efficiency and dynamism of an economy, in a way that transfers unnecessarily to poor individuals. As already mentioned, if there is any rhyme or reason in the prevailing prices, the activities that are making exceptionally high returns are likely to be generating a social surplus, and those that are suffering exceptional losses are likely to be operating at a net loss to the society. Therefore, the value of a society's output will normally be much greater if some resources are shifted from the money-losing to the money-making activities. In a market economy with appropriate institutions, this shift will tend to be brought about automatically by the disparities in the returns. A society that does not shift resources from the losing activities to those that generate a social surplus is irrational, since it is throwing away useful resources in a way that ruins economic performance without the least assurance that it is helping individuals with low incomes. A rational and humane society, then, will confine its distributional transfers to poor and unfortunate individuals.

In this respect, most third-world societies, most Soviet-type societies in the sclerotic stage, and most of the societies that are in transition from communism follow exactly the opposite policies from the ones that should be followed. In many third-world societies, it is commonplace for uneconomic industries and enterprises to be protected and subsidized and for these subsidies to be rationalized on the ostensibly egalitarian grounds that they prevent unemployment of the workers in the uneconomic industry. This policy often exists even when the subsidies support a wage in the uneconomic activity that is several times as high as the average earnings in the society, so the net impact of the subsidies is massively inegalitarian as well as a bar to economic development. In many of the societies in transition from communism, the amount of the (usually implicit) subsidies to uneconomic industry reaches staggering proportions. In the first half of 1992, for example, the increase in interenterprise credit in Russia (apparently mainly funded by the creation of new money) was equal to 70 percent of the half-year's gross domestic product.[10]

The Soviet-type societies usually did not enact national systems of progressive income taxation, unemployment insurance, or many other national safety-net programs that the welfare states of the West have had. They relied in large part on the socialized enterprises for welfare services. They transferred huge amounts of resources from profitable activities to industries, enterprises, and localities whose output was not valuable enough to cover the costs of the resources they utilized. Of course, this type of behavior often occurs in the most prosperous countries of the West as well, but not nearly in such large proportions. What explains this striking difference between the Soviet-type societies and the market democracies? Part of the explanation is the especially insidious sclerosis in the Soviet-type societies that was described earlier. But there is another reason as well.

Individual Rights Reduce Redistributions to Uneconomic Activities

The countries with the highest per-capita incomes—the developed democracies—are also the countries where individual rights are best protected. There are extensive institutional mechanisms to protect individual rights that normally limit the extent to which governmental discretion can be used to prevent the changes in returns and the resource reallocations needed for an efficient and dynamic economy. If individual rights are sufficiently extensive, political and administrative discretion is inevitably limited to some extent.

Suppose there is a large, unexpected increase in demand for the economist's favorite hypothetical product, widgets. Most people in a long-established democracy with markets realize that if Jones happens to be manufacturing widgets when the boom in demand for widgets occurs, then Jones is probably just lucky. But if Jones has acquired his widget factory legally, he will still have a right to the factory's extra profits. This right will be recognized by the courts and protected by the police.

To the extent that individual rights keep the government from capturing the returns in exceptionally profitable enterprises, they also leave the government with fewer resources to dissipate on enterprises that are a drain to the society.

Similarly, the contract holder's right of access to an impartial court means that the lender who makes a secure loan can, if the enterprise to which the loan is made has more costs than revenues and cannot repay the loan, seize the assets of the defaulting borrower. This further reduces the tendency for a society to dissipate resources on activities that subtract from the value of the social output.

The strength of individual rights in longstanding democracies is, therefore, a major explanation of the toleration by these democracies of large variations in short-run rates of return across firms, industries, and localities. This toleration is indispensable for a dynamic and prosperous economy. It provides an incentive for the reallocation of resources from activities where they produce lower rates of return to those where they earn higher rates of return, thereby generating a more nearly rational allocation. It also provides the incentive that makes firms and individuals undertake the inherently risky entrepreneurship needed for the advance of technology and productivity.

A Recapitulation

We have seen that markets are ubiquitous, but that most societies, in spite of their innumerable markets, enjoy neither high incomes nor rapid economic growth. Markets are pervasive in virtually all countries because the gains from trade are normally substantial and sometimes colossal, and because many types of trade are self-enforcing (and accordingly can occur under almost any conditions).

Though arbitrarily fixed prices and other misguided interventions are commonplace, especially in the second and third worlds, societies nonetheless obtain most of the gains from their markets because the transactions that normally provide the smallest gains are blocked by intervention and those that provide the largest gains take place. Thus, virtually the entire world population profits from spontaneous and even irrepressible markets, many of which are in the huge informal sectors in the economies of the second and third worlds. Many markets are largely self-enforcing, in the same way that some lines of production, such as food gathering and handicrafts, are largely self-protected. Self-enforcing markets and self-protected production are extremely valuable: we all gain from them and they keep a large part of the world's population alive.

To achieve rapid economic growth or high levels of income, however, a society needs to obtain gains from the mutually advantageous trades, such as those that involve borrowing and lending and goods purchased for future delivery, that are not self-enforcing. These gains can be obtained only from governmentally or socially contrived markets. A society also needs to gain from rights-intensive production. It needs the gains from property rights–intensive production, such as is necessary whenever production requires extensive use of plants or machinery. It needs the gains from contract rights–intensive production such as that provided by insurance companies, futures markets, and banks. Incomes are low in most of the countries of the world, in short, because the people in those countries do not have secure individual rights.

Well-defined and secure individual rights also make it easier for a society to transfer resources from activities that waste resources to activities that generate net wealth. This is particularly true if the society has a system of social insurance or safety nets that protects unfortunate individuals. Those who have title to assets and enterprises that prove to be unexpectedly profitable in a society with individual rights have a right to the exceptional profits. Just as the winner of a lottery has a right to his or her winnings, so the owner of an unexpectedly profitable asset has, in a rights-based democracy, a right to the exceptional profit even if it is due (as it often is) merely to luck.

These rights to disproportionate profits keep many resources from being shifted to industries or enterprises that subtract from the net output of society. The right to contract enforcement increases the probability that enterprises that subtract from a society's net output will be closed down; lenders have a right to seize the assets that have been promised to them in the event that an enterprise defaults on its secured loans, which is what the enterprise will normally have to do when its costs exceed the value of its output.

Back to the Preface

We now have the theories or tools of thought needed to answer the remaining question posed in the Preface. One of those questions, we recall, was inspired by the low incomes over most of the world, in spite of the ubiquity of the markets that are supposed to bring prosperity. Thus, it was natural to ask how a society can obtain the types of markets that generate the rapid and sustained growth that brings a cornucopia of wealth. If we bring all of the theory and evidence together at once, we see that (if we leave aside a few special conditions that are not important in this context) only two general conditions are required for a market economy that generates economic success.

As we have seen, the first of these conditions is the paradoxical condition of secure and well-defined individual rights.

Rather than being a luxury that only rich countries can afford, individual rights are essential to obtaining the vast gains from the sophisticated transactions described in Chapter 9, and to obtaining the bounteous harvests that property-intensive and contract-intensive production can yield. In particular, a market economy can reach its full potential only if all of the participants in that economy, whether individuals or corporations, native or foreign, have the right to the impartial enforcement of the contracts they choose to make. It may also reach its full potential only if all participants have secure and precisely delineated rights to private property. These rights are never given by nature, but are rather the result of social—and normally governmental—contrivance.

There is no private property without government—individuals may have possessions, the way a dog possesses a bone, but there is private property only if the society protects and defends a private right to that possession against other private parties and against the government as well. If a society has clear and secure individual rights, there are strong incentives to produce, invest, and engage in mutually advantageous trade, and therefore at least some economic advance.

The second condition required for a thriving market economy is simply the absence of predation of any kind. Some predation, such as that which occurs in the war of each against all in a Hobbesian anarchy, or that undertaken when autocrats or other governments abrogate the rights of their subjects by confiscating property or repudiating contracts, is already excluded if the rights hold that are emphasized here, so we do not need to list it separately.

But one other kind of predation can and often does occur even in societies with the best individual rights. This is pre-

dation through lobbying that obtains special-interest legislation or regulation and through cartelization or collusion to fix
prices or wages. As the argument outlined in Chapter 4
shows, collective action to lobby or to fix prices generates a
benefit that goes to everyone in an industry, occupation, or
group, whether or not the individual or firm in question has
made a contribution to the lobbying or price fixing. Because of
this incentive to free ride, it takes a long time for collective
action to emerge in most industries or groups, so only societies that are stable for some time have many coalitions for
collective action. But when a group that constitutes only a
narrow segment of the income-earning capacity of a society is
able to act collectively, its main incentive is to redistribute to
itself through lobbying and price fixing and to continue such
activities even when the losses to the society are large in relation to the amount the group obtains through its distributional struggle. The distortions of prices and the obstacles to
innovation arising from distributional coalitions make an
economy sclerotic.[11] As this book has shown, this sclerotic
process has been taking place in both East and West—I believe
that it occurs in all long-stable societies, whether they are autocratic or democratic.

The two conditions that have just been discussed do not
(without unattainably ideal definitions of rights)[12] guarantee
perfect markets, the maximum socially useful innovation, or
an ideal allocation of resources. Nor do they assure that there
is an income distribution with broad appeal. But I hypothesize
that, given the extraordinary gains available from adopting the
advanced technologies available in the postwar world and the
possibility of interacting with a reasonably successful world
economy, these two conditions, if fully met, are nonetheless

sufficient to bring prosperity to a society. They are sufficient to assure that a society will have not only the markets that exist everywhere but also the full range of markets—including the capital markets that bring foreign investment—that bring even the gains from transactions that are not self-enforcing.

The empirical evidence is overwhelmingly consistent with my hypothesis: the economies that have grown rapidly do not appear to have had perfect markets or ideal arrangements generally—they have been able to grow rapidly in spite of diverse imperfections. There is no society in the postwar world that has fully met the two forgoing conditions that has failed to prosper. An economy that satisfies both of the forgoing conditions is like a boy in early adolescence—there may be many mistakes, but growth is a virtual certainty. Thus I claim to have answered the question, posed in the Preface, of how a society can have not only the markets that almost all societies have but also the markets that are sufficient for a prosperous economy: It need only satisfy the two forgoing conditions.

These two conditions are most likely to be satisfied, I think, in secure, rights-respecting democracies where the institutions are structured in ways that give authoritative decision making as much as possible to encompassing interests. Though lasting democracies (like long-stable societies of any kind) have in the past ultimately come to suffer from narrow special interests, it is by no means inevitable that this must always be true. No historical process that is understood is inevitable.

Narrow special interests are always tiny minorities. If a special-interest group became so large that it represented a majority—or even a very substantial minority—of the society, it would be an encompassing interest and would have relatively constructive incentives. Thus, the problem is that minorities so tiny that they have an incentive to ignore the damage they do to society nonetheless (in part because of the rational ignorance of the mass of the citizenry) are able to influence public policy toward their industry or occupation, or to combine to raise prices or wages in their particular market. But the producers in a particular market are such a tiny minority of the electorate that they cannot get away with this if even the intellectual elite understands what is going on.

It is not impossible that this wider understanding will come to characterize the elites in at least some democracies. There are more than a few people with a professional incentive to study economics or other social sciences, or with some other professional interest in public affairs, and those in such roles will not be rationally ignorant of the public's business. Research and education have some effect, I think, which is one of the reasons why I have written this book. There is also some social learning from experience. The understanding of economics—and maybe the understanding of the logic of institutions and collective choices—seems to have improved a little in the last decade or two. If those of us who are professionally concerned with ideas about how society should be governed—and all of us who are intensely interested in the policies that largely determine how our economies and societies perform—work hard enough and well enough, there may be further understanding.

NOTES

Foreword

1. For an in-depth discussion of these frescoes, see Randolph Stern and Loren Partridge, *Arts of Power*. Berkeley: University of California Press, 1992, pp. 1–80. For a description of the operation of the Commune in Italian cities of this period, see Lauro Martines, *Power and Imagination: City-States in Renaissance Italy*. New York: Knopf, 1979.

2. Note to various scholars about contribution to conference on market-augmenting government. Fall 1997.

3. See, for example, Steven Radelet and Jeffrey Sachs, "The East Asian Financial Crisis: Diagnosis, Remedies, Prospects." Brookings Papers on Economic Activity, January 1998, pp. 2–74.

4. Anthony Lanyi and Young Lee, "Governance Aspects of the East Asian Financial Crisis." Paper presented at the IRIS Conference on Market Augmenting Government, March 1999.

5. Leszek Balcerowicz, *Socialism, Capitalism, Transformation*. Central European University Press, 1995, pp. 160–163.

6. The effort to inform ourselves and participate in the debate is much more costly to us individually than the benefit that would come to us individually from our efforts to reduce the distortion. Thus, it is rational for us to remain ignorant. At the same time, the narrow interests who reap the benefit of all of our individual contributions (through taxes, higher prices, or whatever the particular policy distortion produces) will always have high-powered incentives to organize and importune the government, ignoring the damages to broader society.

7. Dorothy Robyn, *Braking the Special Interests: Trucking Deregulation and the Politics of Policy Reform.* Chicago: The University of Chicago Press, 1987.

8. Jonathan Rauch's *Demosclerosis* (New York: Random House, 1994) builds on Olsonian logic to describe the policy logjam in Washington. His remedies for the problem do not occupy the center of the book but rest in the end on an exasperated public goading politicians to do the right thing, though only after a crisis of dramatic proportion. Examples of reform without crisis are few. Rauch identifies only Thatcher's Great Britain.

9. E-mail to Avanish Dixit, July 1997.

10. The following section traces the evolution of some of Olson's work that is relevant to the present volume. Its main utility will be for those who are not already familiar with Olson's work but would profit from a roadmap to the ideas that are brought together in the book that follows. Its main rationale here is to capture, in his last book, the main works that readers here might find useful. The book stands well on its own, and the following is certainly not necessary to its enjoyment or understanding.

11. Mancur Olson, *The Logic of Collective Action: Public Goods and the Theory of Groups,* Harvard Economic Studies, Volume 124. Cambridge, MA: Harvard University Press, 1965.

12. For a detailed review of Olson's contribution to the understanding of collective action, see Omar Azfar, "The Logic of Collective Action," in the *Elgar Companion to Public Choice, 1999.* Olson's colleague Martin McGuire has written a more personal review of his professional contribution: "Mancur Lloyd Olson Jr. 1932–1998 Personal Recollections." *Eastern Economic Journal.* 24(3), Summer 1998, pp. 253–263.

13. Hardin, Russell, *Collective Action.* Baltimore: Johns Hopkins University Press, 1982; and Todd Sandler, *Collective Action: Theory and Applications.* Ann Arbor: University of Michigan Press, 1992.

14. Mancur Olson, *The Rise and Decline of Nations: Economic Growth, Stagflation and Social Rigidities.* New Haven, CT: Yale University Press, 1982.

15. Mancur Olson, "Diseconomies of Scale and Development, Essays in Honor of Peter Bauer." *Cato Journal* 7(1), Spring/Summer 1987, pp. 77–97.

16. Mancur Olson, "Diseconomies of Scale and Development, Essays in Honor of Peter Bauer." *Cato Journal* 7(1), Spring/Summer 1987, p. 96.

17. Mancur Olson, "Distinguished Lecture on Economics in Government—Big Bills Left on the Sidewalk: Why Some Nations Are Rich, and Others Poor." *Journal of Economic Perspectives* 10(2):3–24 (Spring 1996).

18. In "Does Voluntary Participation Undermine the Coase Theorem?" Forthcoming in the *Journal of Public Economics.* Avanish Dixit and Olson advance a technical argument to assert that simply reducing the transactions costs of political participation will not overcome this tendency. This article, at one point provocatively titled, "The Coase Theorem Is Mostly Wrong," suggests that even very slight costs of collective action make it wrong to extend the Coaseian insight about markets for externalities to political bargaining.

19. Christopher Clague, Philip Keefer, Stephen Knack, and Mancur Olson, "Contract Intensive Money: Contract Enforcement, Property Rights and Economic Performance." *Journal of Economic Growth* 4:185–211 (June 1999); Clague, Keefer, Knack, and Olson, "Property and Contract Rights in Autocracies and Democracies." *Journal of Economic Growth* 1(2):243–276 (June 1996); Mancur Olson, "Dictatorship, Democracy and Development." *American Political Science Review* 87(3):567–576 (September 1993). Also, Martin McGuire and Mancur Olson, "The Economics of Autocracy and Majority Rule: The Invisible Hand and the Use of Force." *Journal of Economic Literature,* March 1996, pp. 72–96.

20. I appreciate and acknowledge comments on this introduction by Omar Azfar, Roger Betancourt, Anthony Lanyi, Peter Murrell, and Alison Olson, but of course its limitations are my responsibility alone.

Chapter One

1. As is well known, this outcome need not be true if market imperfections such as monopoly or monopsony imply that the wage is not equal to the marginal social product. Such imperfections mean that the market would not allocate the ex-criminal's time in a way that is perfectly or Pareto-efficient, but they by no means rule out a very high correlation between the self-interested choices of individuals and firms and gains to society.

2. See, for example, Diego Gambetta, *The Sicilian Mafia.* Cambridge, MA: Harvard University Press, 1993.

3. New Haven and London: Yale University Press, 1982.

4. James E. Sheridan, *Chinese Warlord: The Career of Feng Yu-hsiang.* Stanford: Stanford University Press, 1966.

5. For the sake of tidy and comparable results, I assume that all taxes are linear or flat taxes that take a given percentage of all income, both in the analysis of autocracy and in the account of majoritarian democracy. Later, when discussing the complex and implicit system of taxation that Stalin and his henchmen developed, I consider how the results are changed as the type of taxation changes.

6. Though they did not introduce the concept of an encompassing interest or make the present argument, Ibn Kalduhn (in the fourteenth century) and Joseph Schumpeter (in heavily taxed Austria-Hungary during World War I) pointed out that beyond some point higher tax rates reduce tax collections. See Ibn Kalduhn, *The Muqaddimah, An Introduction to History,* Franz Rosenthal, trans. Princeton, NJ: Princeton University Press, 1989; and Joseph A. Schumpeter, "The Crisis of the Tax State." In Richard Swedberg (ed.), *The Economics and Sociology of Capitalism.* Princeton, NJ: Princeton University Press, 1991.

7. How does the stationary bandit rate of tax theft compare with the total rate of theft extraction when there is both a Mafia family and a stationary bandit? If there is both a Mafia family and a maximizing autocrat extracting resources, the combined protection racket tax plus autocrat's tax will be higher than if only one of them has been taxing. When the Mafia leader, for example, is deciding on

the protection racket charge and is aware that activity in the neighborhood is curtailed by the protection charge, he notes that some of the loss takes the form of lower governmental tax collections, and the Mafia family has no incentive to take this loss into account in deciding on the rate of protection payment it demands. If a Mafia family were, like our bandit gang that settles down, strong enough so that its protection racket charge were the only tax, then the aggregate tax rate imposed on citizens would be lower and the income of the neighborhood would be higher. That is, competition among autocratic rulers for power over the same domain is bad for the subjects and monopoly by a single ruler is better for them.

8. The deadweight losses from the tax theft increase—probably more than proportionally—with the rate of tax theft. Then the faster (slower) the deadweight losses rise with increases in the tax rate, the lower (higher) the optimal tax rate must be for the stationary bandit. It is, however, possible that the deadweight loss function could have an irregular shape that would keep the foregoing proposition from holding. To focus on what I think are the most probable situations— and to achieve maximum simplicity—I assume throughout that the deadweight losses from taxation rise steadily and more than proportionally with the tax rate. For the second-order conditions for maxima in the argument, see the article by Martin C. McGuire and Mancur Olson, "The Economics of Autocracy and Majority Rule: The Invisible Hand and the Use of Force." *Journal of Economic Literature* 34:72 (March 1996).

9. Though the tax collections at each rate of tax theft vary with the level of public good provision, the optimal or revenue-maximizing rate should not, and that is what I assume. Thus, the stationary bandit first chooses his optimal rate of tax theft, thereby determining the share of the benefits of public goods that he receives, and then chooses the level of public good provision that is optimal for him.

10. The outcome is different when a public good increases the quality of life but does not add to production and taxable income. For example, if abatement of air pollution made life more pleasant but had no effect, through the health of workers, on taxable output, the stationary bandit would not spend resources on it, except to the

extent that he lived in the same airspace as his subjects. To avoid complications that would add little or no insight, I assume in this book that all public goods are producers' public goods—that is, inputs in the productive process that are equally necessary to the production of any and all income.

11. Martin C. McGuire and Mancur Olson, "The Economics of Autocracy and Majority Rule: The Invisible Hand and the Use of Force." *Journal of Economic Literature* 34:72 (March 1996).

12. As the next chapter explains, many of the more remarkable examples of economic progress and the advance of civilization even in historic times took place in somewhat democratic or nondictatorial societies such as ancient Athens, the Roman Republic, the northern Italian city-states, the Netherlands in the seventeenth century, and in Great Britain after the Glorious Revolution of 1688–89. Significant economic progress in the nineteenth century occurred in the United States and other societies with representative rather than autocratic government.

13. In the analysis of democracies, we shall find some majorities so encompassing that they have an incentive to act in total accord with the interests of society.

14. Robert E. Quirk, *Fidel Castro.* New York: Norton, 1993, p. 625.

15. When the ruling interest includes everyone in the society, the share of income that it receives is not a fraction but all: one or 100 percent. Though the reciprocal rule still applies (because $1/1 = 1$), it now tells us nothing new: it is just another way of stating the familiar point from economic theory that a society that takes everyone into account and maximizes total welfare will spend on public goods until the marginal social cost of the public goods equals the marginal social benefits. The ruling interest that includes everyone obviously also will not redistribute anything to itself: by raising taxes beyond the level needed to fund public goods and distributing the surplus to itself, it would suffer losses from incentive-distorting taxation with no return. (If such a society unanimously agreed to redistribute income to, say, its poorer members, that redistribution would be a public good and should not be analyzed the way that self-interested redistribution through the use of political power is analyzed.) Inter-

estingly, this situation also applies to the superencompassing majorities considered later in this chapter.

16. That is, the only objection that could be made to the social outcome concerns the distribution of initial endowments or capacities to earn income. Given the initial endowments, it is not possible to make anyone better off without making someone else worse off.

17. Some mistakenly suppose that a continuing "head" tax—pay the fixed tax or you lose your head—is a lump-sum tax. If the tax continues, it can be collected only if the threats to behead are credible and thus sometimes carried out. But this punishment (like the head tax itself) not only affects the incentive that taxpayers have to flee to another jurisdiction but also reduces the number of producers and taxpayers. Thus, even this tax changes incentives and the level of output.

18. Because the incentive to produce tends to disappear under anarchy, it is assumed that public goods are necessary to generate any and all income.

19. William A. Niskanen, "Autocratic, Democratic, and Optimal Government." *Economic Inquiry* 35:464–479 (July 1997).

Chapter Two

1. If an autocrat's tax rate is less than 50 percent, so more than half of the return from capital goes to the private owner, the capital value of a capital good will necessarily exceed the discounted present value of its tax yield. In some autocracies, this can make private property rights in capital goods even less secure than they would otherwise be. I am thankful to Yew-Kwang Ng for bringing this important point to my attention. Even so, an autocrat with a sufficiently long time horizon would not necessarily be rational to confiscate capital goods, since this would reduce investment and perhaps deprive him of the gains that came from the income generated by a succession of private investments.

2. When war erodes confidence about what the boundaries of an autocrat's domain will be, an autocrat's time horizon with respect to

his possession of any given territory shortens, even if he believes he will remain in control of some territory somewhere. In the limit, complete uncertainty about what territory an autocrat will control implies roving banditry. The advantages of stationary over roving banditry are obviously greatest when there are natural and militarily defensible frontiers. Interestingly, the earliest states in history emerged mainly in what one anthropologist called "environmentally circumscribed" areas, that is, areas of arable land surrounded by deserts, mountains, or coasts (see Robert L. Carniero's "A Theory of the Origin of the State." *Science* 169:733–738 [1970]). The environmental circumscription not only provides militarily viable frontiers but also (as Carniero points out) limits the opportunity for defeated tribes to flee to other areas in which they could support themselves. In turn, the consensual democracy characteristic of the earliest stages of social evolution is in these geographical conditions replaced by autocratic states earlier than in other conditions.

3. Some undemocratic regimes can institutionalize succession, but then they are not under the exclusive control of a single autocrat and are more nearly oligarchies. This is true even if the regimes are in some degree totalitarian. After the death of Stalin, the government of the Soviet Union came to be routinized, and then the succession to the leadership was determined, albeit by very small groups, according to institutional rules. But when politburos or other multiperson bodies have the power to determine the successor to a leader, they also limit his power, or even depose him (as was done with Khrushchev).

4. *Capitalism, Socialism and Democracy*, 4th ed. London: Allen and Unwin, 1954.

5. David Lake, "Powerful Pacifists: Democratic States and War." *American Political Science Review* 86:24–37 (1992).

6. Robert A. Dahl, *Polyarchy: Participation and Opposition.* New Haven, CT: Yale University Press, 1971; and Tatu Vanhanen, "The Level of Democratization Related to Socioeconomic Variables in 147 States in 1980–85." *Scandinavian Political Studies* 12(2):95–127 (1989).

7. The units under the command of military officers are normally segregated in separate barracks. This, and the typically hierarchical character of military organizations, makes it less likely that military juntas, even if there is a balance of power among the officers of which they are comprised, will evolve into democracies.

8. Strictly speaking, there is also a fourth necessary condition, but its logic will not be evident until we deal with the logic of collective action. The condition is that the number of different parties who must arrange for power-sharing arrangements must be small enough for voluntary collective action to take place. If there are, say, thousands of different families with similar degrees of power, voluntary collective action cannot, for the reasons that are explained later, succeed in obtaining the gains from a peaceful order and the provision of other public goods. Then there will be anarchy that will last until someone acquires enough power to become a stationary bandit. The number of leaders who must agree to form a nonautocratic government must be comparable to the number of families in an acephalous or consensually governed band or tribe.

9. "Autocratic, Democratic, and Optimal Government." *Economic Inquiry* 35:464–479 (July 1997).

10. Avner Greif, "On the Political Foundations of the Late Medieval Commercial Revolution: Genoa During the Twelfth and Thirteenth Centuries." *Journal of Economic History* 54(2):271–287 (June 1994).

11. Christopher Hibbert, *Venice: The Biography of a City.* New York and London: W. W. Norton and Company, 1989, p. 49. I am grateful to Philip Coelho for bringing this example to my attention.

12. Bradford J. DeLong and Andrei Shleifer, "Princes and Merchants: European City Growth Before the Industrial Revolution." *Journal of Law and Economics* 36(2):671–702 (October 1993).

13. James Madison, *The Papers of James Madison,* Robert A. Rutland, Thomas A. Mason, Robert J. Brugger, Jeanne K. Sisson, and Fredrika J. Teute (eds.). Charlottesville: University Press of Virginia, 1983.

14. Christopher Clague, Philip Keefer, Stephen Knack, and Mancur Olson, "Property and Contract Rights in Autocracies and Democracies." *Journal of Economic Growth* 1(2): 243–276 (June 1996).

Chapter Three

1. These two articles are "The Nature of the Firm." *Economica*, pp. 386–405 (November 1937); and "The Problem of Social Cost." *Journal of Law and Economics* 3:1–44 (October 1960).

2. See, for example, Oliver Williamson, *The Economic Institutions of Capitalism*. New York: The Free Press, 1985.

3. This must be the social loss after the victims have adjusted efficiently to the damage. If the victims are fully compensated for the losses they incur, they will have no incentive to minimize these losses and the result will not be socially efficient (see Mancur Olson Jr. and Richard Zeckhauser, "The Efficient Production of External Economies." *American Economic Review* 60(3):512–517 (June 1970).

4. A. C. Pigou, *The Economics of Welfare*, 4th ed. London: Macmillan, 1946.

5. See, for example, Douglass C. North, "A Transactions Cost Theory of Government." *Journal of Theoretical Politics* 2(4):355. Avinash Dixit's "The Making of Economic Policy: A Transaction-Cost Politics Perspective" (*Munich Lectures in Economics*. Cambridge and London: MIT Press, pp. xvii, 192) also offers a transactions cost theory of economic policymaking within an existing framework of governance, thereby explicitly abstracting from the problems that are explained in this book.

6. "A Theory of Competition Among Pressure Groups for Political Influence." *Quarterly Journal of Economics* 106:407–443 (May 1991); and "Public Policies, Pressure Groups, and Dead Weight Costs." *Journal of Public Economics* 28:329–347 (December 1985). For a leading example of the application of the Becker model, see Bruce Gardner, "Efficient Redistribution Through Commodity

Markets." *American Journal of Agricultural Economics* 65(2):225–234 (May 1983).

7. For interesting studies that can instructively be considered along this line, whether they explicitly use the transactions cost approach to government or politics or not, see George J. Stigler, "The Theory of Economic Regulation." *Bell Journal of Economics and Management Science* 2:3–21 (Spring 1971); and "Law or Economics?" *Journal of Law and Economics* 35(2):455–468 (October 1992); Earl Thompson and Roger Faith, "A Pure Theory of Strategic Behavior and Social Institutions." *American Economic Review* 71(3):366–380 (June 1981); Donald Wittman, "Why Democracies Produce Efficient Results." *Journal of Political Economy* 97(6):1395–1424 (1989); Gary Becker, *The Myth of Democratic Failure: Why Political Institutions Are Efficient.* Chicago: University of Chicago Press, 1995. The aforementioned articles by Gary Becker are also pertinent here.

8. Though there must always be a peaceful agreement that would leave both parties better off, it is not always the case that this agreement is self-enforcing. If it is not, as Donald Wittman has correctly pointed out, there may be no impartial third party that will enforce the agreement ("Why Democracies Produce Efficient Results." *Journal of Political Economy* 97(6):1395–1424). Though there are international tribunals and courts, they often do not have the power to make countries abide by their agreements.

9. "Big Bills Left on the Sidewalk: Why Some Countries Are Rich and Others Poor." *Journal of Economic Perspectives (U.S.)* 10:3–24 (Spring 1996).

10. *Arms and Influence.* New Haven, CT: Yale University Press, 1966, p. v.

11. "The Dark Side of the Force." Presidential Address to the Western Economics Association. *Economic Inquiry* 32:1–10 (January 1994).

12. "The Making of Economic Policy: A Transaction-Cost Politics Perspective." *Munich Lectures in Economics.* Cambridge and London: MIT Press, pp. xvii, 192.

Chapter Four

1. Cambridge: Harvard University Press, 1965.
2. Baltimore, MD: John Hopkins University Press, 1982.
3. Ann Arbor, MI: University of Michigan Press, 1992.
4. It is true that the provision will not be group optimal if there is a beneficiary who does not participate, which means that the non-participant also will obtain less of the collective good than if he or she shared the costs. If the group is so small that there are only two or a few beneficiaries of the collective good, this could motivate participation: the gains from obtaining more could be so great that it could be better to share the costs of all units and obtain a larger quantity than to be a free rider with a smaller provision. In the large groups that are at issue now, this consideration almost never applies. In a group of a thousand, if one average beneficiary is free riding, that individual's participation will add only about one-thousandth to the value of the provision, and will thus motivate only a trivial increase in provision. One or a few typical individuals in a large group will add so little to the provision by participating that this increment will scarcely affect their welfare. Their share of the cost of all of the units provided may not, however, be at all trivial to them. Thus, the typical individual in a large group is normally better off free riding on a trivially suboptimal supply than paying an appropriate share of the cost of all units provided.

5. Some might argue that an entrepreneur would circulate a proposed agreement that each party would pay his or her share of the cost of the collective good, but that the agreement would go into effect only if all of the potential beneficiaries signed it. But if unanimous consent is required, it would pay an individual to be a holdout. The holdout could then agree to sign only if he or she received a large share of the gains from consummation of the agreement! The others could gain from giving in to this demand, rather than let the stipulation of unanimity and the holdout keep them from achieving all of the gain of provision. If the contract does not require unanimous consent for provision, the holdout might simply refuse to bear any of the costs of the collective good, knowing that the others will

gain from going ahead by themselves. If bargains are enforceable and those who design agreements intended to obtain group optimality are given the first move, it is possible to design agreements that will obtain provision. But this requires giving an arbitrary first-move advantage to efficient outcomes. If the same arbitrary advantage is given to anyone who could gain from being a free rider, there will in general be no possibility of group-optimal voluntary provision, even if the cost of the resources devoted to the bargaining are met from the outside.

6. "Does Voluntary Participation Undermine the Coase Theorem?" *Elsevier Science S.A. Economic Letters* 61, 3–11.

7. The word *large* is used loosely here in order to avoid going into a great variety of cases that do not need to be examined to refute the Coase theorem. Games without cores could also arise in smaller groups, especially when there is what I called the "exploitation of the great by the small" in *The Logic of Collective Action*—that is, in cases where one party places a much higher absolute value on the public good than others in the group do.

Chapter Five

1. There is quantitative evidence from an exhaustive survey of ethnographic accounts showing that references to slaves are virtually absent in the accounts of most primitive peoples but are rather common in more advanced agricultural societies (see L. T. Hobhouse, G. C. Wheeler, and M. Ginsberg, *The Material Culture and Social Institutions of the Simpler Peoples.* London: Routledge and Kegan Paul, 1965; and the demonstration of the unprofitability of slavery in hunting-gathering societies in Mancur Olson Jr., "Some Historic Variation in Property Institutions," Princeton University. Mimeo, 1967).

2. Small tribes can sometimes form federations and thereby increase the number of those who can obtain collective goods through voluntary action (Mancur Olson Jr., *The Logic of Collective Action.* Cambridge, MA: Harvard University Press, 1965, pp. 62–63). Some

of the very earliest agricultural societies may have been of this character. But when the number of small groups itself becomes very large, voluntary collective action is infeasible.

3. New Haven and London: Yale University Press, 1982.

4. See, for example, Kwang Choi, *Theories of Economic Growth.* Ames, IA: Iowa State University Press, 1983; Richard Vedder and Lowell Galloway, "Rentseeking, Distributional Coalitions, Taxes, Relative Prices, and Economic Growth." *Public Choice* 51(1):93–100 (1986); Steve Chan, "Growth with Equity: A Test of Olson's Theory for the Asian Pacific-Rim Countries." *Journal of Peace Research* 24(2):135–149 (1987); Erich Weede, "Catch-Up, Distributional Coalitions and Government as Determinants of Growth and Decline in Industrial Democracies." *British Journal of Sociology* 37:194–220 (1986); Jan-Erik Lane and Svante Ersson, *Comparative Political Economy.* London and New York: Pinter, distributed by Columbia University Press, 1990, pp. viii, 296; Todd Sandler, *Collective Action: Theory and Applications.* Ann Arbor: University of Michigan Press, 1992; Jonathan Rauch, *Demosclerosis.* New York: Times Books, 1994; and many of the contributions in Dennis C. Mueller, ed., *The Political Economy of Growth.* New Haven, CT: Yale University Press, 1983; *International Studies Quarterly* 27 (1983); *Scandinavian Political Studies* 9 (March 1986).

5. Christopher Clague, Philip Keefer, Stephen Knack, and Mancur Olson, "Property and Contract Rights in Autocracies and Democracies." *Journal of Economic Growth* 1(2):243–276 (June 1996). As we have seen earlier, this article also provides compelling statistical evidence that property and contract rights are on average much better in the lasting democracies than in any other types of regime.

Chapter Seven

1. In the very short run, just after the collectivization of agriculture and other productive assets, there was apparently a period of "indigestion" and confusion when output may have significantly declined. But for most of the rest of Stalin's reign, the output that

Stalin cared about was far higher than it had been before he imposed Stalinization on the USSR.

2. See Ronald I. McKinnon, "Taxation, Money, and Credit in a Liberalizing Socialist Economy." In Christopher Clague and Gordon Rausser (eds.), *The Emergence of Market Economies in Eastern Europe.* Cambridge, MA, and Oxford: Blackwell, 1992, pp. 109–127.

3. There are special cases, for example, fixed costs of each employee, or the transactions costs for employers in hiring temporary employees, that sometimes generate a range of progressivity in piece rates in a market economy. But these considerations are presumably not of much relevance to the present argument.

4. Peter Gatrell and Mark Harrison, "The Russian and Soviet Economies in Two World Wars: A Comparative View." *Economic History Review* 46:444 (August 1993).

5. The army of the Austro-Hungarian Empire was also used against tsarist Russia, but this army was often said to be poorer than that of any other combatant country in World War I, and it did not play an impressive role in the defeat of Russia.

6. Gatrell and Harrison, Table 9 and pp. 425–452. Gatrell and Harrison point out that, "In World War I . . . only Germany's failure to disentangle itself from the Western front prevented the speedy victory over Russia which Germany intended. Even so, a small fraction of Germany's military power was able eventually to bring about Russia's defeat and disintegration. In the second war . . . the scale of Soviet mobilization, when combined with overwhelming economic superiority of the Allies, was sufficient to destroy Germany completely as a military power . . . the USSR made a contribution . . . that was disproportionate to the size and level of development of the Soviet economy" (p. 438).

7. William Easterly and Stanley Fischer, "Soviet Economic Decline: Historical and Republican Data." National Bureau of Economic Research, Working Paper Series No. 4735:1–[563] (1994).

8. Peter Murrell and Mancur Olson, "The Devolution of Centrally Planned Economies." *Journal of Comparative Economics* 15:239–265 (1991).

Chapter Eight

1. Because it is impossible for a bureaucracy to make decisions about all of the countless goods and services produced in a vast economy, innumerable decisions were in fact left for negotiations and contracts among state enterprises and to diverse legal, informal, and black markets.

2. When prices were too low to clear the market, as they so often were, the receiving enterprise would be more dependent on the choices of the provider enterprise, which would reduce the receiving enterprise's incentive to report the shortcomings of its supplier. I am indebted to Peter Murrell for calling this point to my attention.

3. Heidi Kroll, "The Role of Contracts in the Soviet Economy." *Soviet Studies* 40:349–366 (July 1988). There is also a valuable analysis in Kroll's article of arbitration of both precontract and contract disputes, and an intriguing account of Soviet arbitration and courts in Harold Berman, *Justice in the USSR: An Interpretation of Soviet Law.* Cambridge, MA: Harvard University Press, 1963.

4. Independent Communist party representatives in enterprises, as distinguished from the official administrators of the enterprises, augmented the regular bureaucratic competition and further improved the information available to the leadership. The party representatives in a factory operated to some extent in the way the inspectorate or censorial system in imperial China worked, increasing the effectiveness of bureaucratic competition in controlling the incentives of subordinates to submit biased information.

5. I am thankful to Laurent Martin for bringing this point to my attention.

6. Clifford G. Gaddy, "Pretending to Work and Pretending to Pay: A Hedonic Wage Approach to the Behavior of Soviet Workers and Managers," in *The Labor Market and the Second Economy in the Soviet Union,* Occasional Paper No. 24, Berkeley-Duke Occasional Papers on the Second Economy in the USSR, Duke University, January 1991.

7. *How the Soviet Union Is Governed.* Cambridge, MA: Harvard University Press, 1979, pp. 446–448.

8. "Poland: Roots of Economic Crisis." *ACES Bulletin* 24:12–14 (1982).

9. "Institutions and the Transition to a Market Economy." In Christopher Clague and Gordon Rausser (eds.), *The Emergence of Market Economies in Eastern Europe*. Cambridge, MA, and Oxford: Basil Blackwell, 1992, pp. 301–310.

10. "Integration of Special Interests into the Hungarian Economy." *Journal of Comparative Economics* 15:284–303 (1991).

11. Given the foregoing logic, there is nothing puzzling in the fact that Soviet-type regimes normally required state enterprises to make all payments through the state banking system and whenever possible tried to keep enterprises from using or holding currency. This facilitated extraction by the center and made retention of profits by the enterprise more difficult.

The multiplication of private firms after the collapse of communism means that there are more enterprises that use significant amounts of currency. These private firms are subject to extortion by Mafia gangs in ways that state-owned enterprises without cash are not. This consideration has probably helped make Mafia-type crime increase in many countries after the collapse of communism. The disorganization attendant upon the collapse of the old order has probably worked in the same direction. The emergence of a free press has greatly improved the reportage of crime and made it more visible. Thus, there are a number of factors that increase crime and make it more visible after the collapse of communism. They do not, as I see it, alter the more fundamental reality that official corruption and widespread crime are a natural legacy of Stalin's extraordinary system of implicit tax collection.

Chapter Nine

1. George Akerlof, Andrew Rose, Janet Yellin, and Helga Hessenius, "East Germany in from the Cold: The Economic Aftermath of Currency Union." *Brookings Papers on Economic Activity* 1:1–87 (1991). The policy conclusions that these authors

draw from their results is, it should be emphasized, very different from those that make sense if the argument in this book is correct.

2. Anne O. Krueger, "Institutions for the New Private Sector." In Christopher Clague and Gordon Rausser (eds.), *The Emergence of Market Economies in Eastern Europe.* Oxford: Basil Blackwell, 1992, pp. 219–223.

3. *New York Times,* June 20, 1993, p. F7; and *The Economist,* August 14, 1993, p. 71.

4. "Why Economic Reforms Fail in the Soviet System." *Economic Inquiry* 28:195–221 (1990).

Chapter Ten

1. There is a vast quantitative literature that supposes that the per-capita incomes of countries are what they are because it is impossible to generate more income in each country from the available resources and technology. Each country is on the frontier of its aggregate production function and its income is as high as it can be, given the available resources. I have shown in "Big Bills Left on the Sidewalk: Why Some Countries Are Rich and Others Poor" (*Journal of Economic Perspectives* 10:3–24 [Spring 1996]) that the low- and middle-income societies are not remotely near the frontiers of their aggregate production functions, so their available natural and human resources cannot explain their low incomes. So aggregate production function (or sources of growth) literature, valuable as it is in some respects, does not resolve the paradox.

2. See P. J. H. Grierson, *The Silent Trade.* Edinburgh: William Greene and Sons, 1903.

3. Simon Katzenellenbogen of the University of Pennsylvania.

4. He set out his findings in "Informal Income Opportunities and Urban Employment in Ghana." *Journal of Modern African Studies* (March 1973).

5. *The Other Path: The Invisible Revolution in the Third World.* New York: Harper & Row, 1989; first published in Spanish.

6. In Figure 10.1, Quantity Q_e will be traded at the market clearing price. Either price p' or p'' will lead to exactly half as much trade, $Q_e/2$. The reduction in the gain from trade is the triangle ABC, and it is immediately obvious that, if demand curves must slope downward and supply curves upward, this loss must be decidedly less than half of the total gain from trade at the equilibrium price, area ADO. Though randomly chosen prices that allow any trade at all to occur will not generate such an outcome very often, it is obviously possible to choose prices that will eliminate most of the gains from trade, such as those that reduce trade to $Q_e/10$.

7. When a good is overpriced, there will tend to be exceptional profits in producing it, and some resources will be devoted to the competition for the right to produce it. That is, there will, in general, be "rent seeking" to obtain the exceptional returns that tend to be associated with price or quantity distortions. The social waste from this rent seeking makes the loss from distorting prices and quantities greater than they would otherwise be. It is sometimes suggested that the resources devoted to rent seeking will equal or approach the amount of the rents. The empirical evidence indicates, however, that the expenditures on rent seeking are normally very small in relation to the size of the rents. This should not be a surprise: we know from analyzing collective action that the logic of free riding works against competitive rent seeking on a given side of any market, so monopoly in rent seeking in each market is the most common situation. This monopoly in rent seeking greatly limits the amount of resources dissipated. Accordingly, the conclusion that, with price or quantity distortions, the losses in gains from trade normally diminish less than the quantity of trading, continues to hold.

8. This argument does not hold in certain classes of cases in the very long run, when (as often happens) the price distortions arise because of cartels, or lobbies that obtain governmentally enforced output quotas or regulations that are functionally similar to cartelization. In these cases, the quantity restrictions lower the rate of innovation and productivity increase that is, in a rapidly growing economy, the most important source of economic growth. Though I have not yet completed the papers that spell out this possibility

fully, I have discussed several aspects of it in my book on *How Bright Are the Northern Lights? Some Questions About Sweden* (Lund, Sweden: Institute of Economic Research, Lund University Press, 1990).

9. In "Why Some Welfare-State Redistribution to the Poor Is a Great Idea" and in the technical articles cited in that piece (which is in Charles K. Rowley, ed., *Public Choice and Liberty: Essays in Honor of Gordon Tullock.* Oxford: Basil Blackwell, 1986).

10. David Lipton and Jeffrey Sachs, "Prospects for Russia's Economic Reforms." *Brookings Papers on Economic Activity*, n2, p. 213, 1992.

11. Societies do, of course, make many mistakes in economic policy besides those inspired by special interests, but societies do (however slowly) also learn. Thus, they will not persevere in economic policies that are fatal to economic growth if there are no organized interests that gain from these economic policies.

12. I bypass the problems of environmental pollution and other externalities that are at the center of many of my other writings but would be merely a distraction here by assuming that the property rights and other individual rights described above are defined to eliminate externalities. Of course, this crowds many complex and important problems into the definitions of a few words, and thus, for most purposes, would not be satisfactory.

BIBLIOGRAPHY

Akerlof, Andrew Rose, Janet Yellin, and Helga Hessenious. 1991. "East Germany in from the Cold: The Economic Aftermath of Currency Union." *Brookings Papers on Economc Activity* 1:1–87.

Becker, Gary. 1995. *The Myth of Democratic Failure: Why Political Institutions Are Efficient.* Chicago: University of Chicago Press.

Berman, Harold. 1963. *Justice in the USSR: An Interpretation of Soviet Law.* Cambridge, MA: Harvard University Press.

Carniero, Robert L. 1970. "A Theory of the Origin of the State." *Science* 169:733–738.

Chan, Steve. 1987. "Growth with Equity: A Test of Olson's Theory for the Asian Pacific-Rim Countries." *Journal of Peace Research* 24(2):135–149.

Choi, Kwang. 1983. *Theories of Economic Growth.* Ames, IA: Iowa State University Press.

Coase, Ronald. November 1937. "The Nature of the Firm." *Economica,* pp. 386–405.

Coase, Ronald. October 1960. "The Problem of Social Cost." *Journal of Law and Economics* 3:1–44.

Clague, Christopher, Philip Keefer, Stephen Knack, and Mancur Olson. June 1996. "Property and Contract Rights in Autocracies and Democracies." *Journal of Economic Growth* 1(2):243–276.

Dahl, Robert A. 1971. *Polyarchy: Participation and Opposition.* New Haven, CT: Yale University Press.

DeLong, Bradford J., and Andrei Shleifer. October 1993. "Princes and Merchants: European City Growth Before the Industrial Revolution." *Journal of Law and Economics* 36(2):671–702.

DeSoto, Hernando. 1989. *The Other Path: The Invisible Revolution in the Third World.* New York: Harper & Row.

Dixit, Avinash. 1996. "The Making of Economic Policy: A Transaction-Cost Politics Perspective." In *Munich Lectures in Economics.* Cambridge and London: MIT Press, pp. xvii, 192.

Dixit, Avinash, and Mancur Olson. 1998. "Does Voluntary Participation Undermine the Coase Theorem?" *Elsevier Science S.A. Economic Letters* 61, 3–11.

Easterly, William, and Stanley Fischer. 1994. "The Soviet Economic Decline: Historical and Republican Data." National Bureau of Economic Research, Working Paper Series No. 4735: 1–[56].

Economic Inquiry 33 (January 1994). "The Dark Side of the Force." Presidential Address to the Western Economics Association, pp. 1–10.

The Economist. August 14, 1993. "How to Start an Airline with $5,000." Business, Finance and Science. U.K. Editions, p. 71.

Gaddy, Clifford G. January 1991. "Pretending to Work and Pretending to Pay: A Hedonic Wage Approach to the Behavior of Soviet Workers and Managers." In *The Labor Market and the Second Economy in the Soviet Union,* Occasional Paper No. 24, Berkeley-Duke Occasional Papers on the Second Economy in the USSR, Duke University, January 1991.

Gambetta, Diego. 1993. *The Sicilian Mafia.* Cambridge, MA: Harvard University Press.

Gardner, Bruce. May 1983. "Efficient Redistribution Through Commodity Markets." *American Journal of Agricultural Economics* 65(2):225–234.

Gatrell, Peter, and Mark Harrison. August 1993. "The Russian and Soviet Economies in Two Worlds Wars: A Comparative View." *Economic History Review* 46:425–452.

Greif, Avner. June 1994. "On the Political Foundations of the Late Medieval Commercial Revolution: Genoa During the Twelfth and Thirteenth Centuries." *Journal of Economic History* 54(2): 271–287.

Grierson, P. J. H. 1903. *The Silent Trade.* Edinburgh: William Greene and Sons.

Hardin, Russell. 1982. *Collective Action.* Baltimore, MD: Johns Hopkins University Press.

Hart, Keith. March 1973. "Informal Income Opportunities and Urban Employment in Ghana." *Journal of Modern African Studies.*

Herodotus. 1987. *The History of Herodotus.* Translated by David Grene. Chicago: University of Chicago Press.

Hibbert, Christopher. 1989. *Venice: The Biography of a City.* New York and London: W. W. Norton & Company, p. 49.

Hobhouse, L. T., G. C. Wheeler, and M. Ginsberg. 1965. *The Material Culture and Social Institutions of the Simpler Peoples.* London: Routledge and Kegan Paul.

Hough, Jerry, and Merle Fainsod. 1979. *How the Soviet Union Is Governed.* Cambridge, MA: Harvard University Press, pp. 446–448.

International Studies Quarterly, vol. 27. Oxford: Blackwell Publishers, 1983.

Journal of Public Economics. December 1985. "Public Policies, Pressure Groups, and Dead Weight Costs," pp. 329–347.

Kalduhn, Ibn. 1989. *The Muqaddimah, an Introduction to History,* translated by Franz Rosenthal. Princeton, NJ: Princeton University Press, pp. 230–231.

Kroll, Heidi. July 1988. "The Role of Contracts in the Soviet Economy." *Soviet Studies* 40:349–366.

Krueger, Anne O. 1992. "Institutions of the New Private Sector." In Christopher Clague and Gordon Rausser (eds.), *The Emergence of Market Economies in Eastern Europe.* Oxford: Basil Blackwell, pp. 219–223.

Lake, David. 1992. "Powerful Pacifists: Democratic States and War." *American Political Science Review* 86:24–37.

Lane, Jan-Erik, and Svante Ersson. 1990. *Comparative Political Economy.* London and New York: Pinter; distributed by Columbia University Press, New York, pp. viii, 296.

Lipton, David, and Jeffrey Sachs. 1992. "Prospects for Russia's Economic Reforms." *Brookings Papers on Economic Activity* 2:213.

Madison, James. 1983. *The Papers of James Madison,* Robert A. Rutland, Thomas A. Mason, Robert J. Brugger, Jeanne K. Sisson, and Fredrika J. Teute (eds.). Charlottesville: University of Virginia Press.

McGuire, Martin C., and Mancur Olson. March 1996. "The Economics of Autocracy and Majority Rule: The Invisible Hand and the Use of Force." *Journal of Economic Literature* 34:72.

McKinnon, Ronald I. 1992. "Taxation, Money, and Credit in a Liberalizing Socialist Economy." In Christopher Clague and Gordon Rausser (eds.), *The Emergence of Market Economies in Eastern Europe.* Cambridge, MA, and Oxford: Basil Blackwell, pp. 109–127.

Montias, Michael. 1982. "Poland: Roots of Economic Crisis." *ACES Bulletin* 24:12–14.

Mueller, Dennis C., ed. 1983. *The Political Economy of Growth.* New Haven, Yale University Press.

Murrell, Peter, and Mancur Olson. 1991. "The Devolution of Centrally Planned Economies." *Journal of Comparative Economics* 15:239–265.

Nagy, Andras. 1992. "Institutions and the Transition to a Market Economy." In Christopher Clague and Gordon Rausser (eds.), *The Emergence of Market Economies in Eastern Europe.* Cambridge, MA, and Oxford: Basil Blackwell, pp. 301–310.

Niskanen, William A. 1997. "Autocratic, Democratic and Optimal Government." *Economic Inquiry* 35:464–479.

North, Douglass C. 1990. A Transactions Cost Theory of Government. *Journal of Theoretical Politics* 2(4):355–367.

Olson, Mancur, Jr. 1965. *The Logic of Collective Action.* Cambridge, MA: Harvard University Press.

Olson, Mancur, Jr. 1967. "Some Historic Variation in Property Institutions." Princeton University. Mimeo.

Olson, Mancur, Jr. 1982. *The Rise and Decline of Nations.* New Haven and London: Yale University Press.

Olson, Mancur, Jr. 1986. "Why Some Welfare-State Redistribution to the Poor Is a Great Idea." In Charles K. Rowley (ed.), *Public Choice and Liberty: Essays in Honor of Gordon Tullock.* Oxford: Basil Blackwell.

Olson, Mancur, Jr. 1990. *How Bright Are the Northern Lights? Some Questions About Sweden.* Lund, Sweden: Institute of Economic Research, Lund University Press.

Olson, Mancur, Jr. Spring 1996. "Big Bills Left on the Sidewalk: Why Some Countries Are Rich and Others Poor." *Journal of Economic Perspectives (U.S.)* 10:3–24.

Olson, Mancur, Jr., and Richard Zeckhauser. June 1970. "The Efficient Production of External Economies." *American Economic Review* 60(3):512–517.

Perlez, Jane. June 20, 1993. "Poland's New Entrepreneurs Push the Economy Ahead." *New York Times.*

Pigou, A. C. *The Economics of Welfare,* 4th ed. London: Macmillan, 1946.

Quarterly Journal of Economics. May 1991. "A Theory of Competition Among Pressure Groups for Political Influence," pp. 407–443.

Quirk, Robert E. 1993. *Fidel Castro.* New York: Norton. p. 625.

Rauch, Jonathan. 1994. *Demosclerosis.* New York: Time Books.

Sandler, Todd. 1992. *Collective Action: Theory and Appications.* Ann Arbor: University of Michigan Press.

Scandinavian Political Studies, vol. 9. Oxford: Blackwell Publishers. March 1986.

Schelling, Thomas. 1966. *Arms and Influence.* New Haven, CT: Yale University Press, p. v.

Schumpeter, Joseph. 1976. *Capitalism, Socialism and Democracy,* 4th ed. London: Allen and Unwin.

Schumpeter, Joseph A. 1991. "The Crisis of the Tax State." In Richard Swedberg (ed.), *The Economics and Sociology of Capitalism.* Princeton, NJ: Princeton University Press, pp. 99–140.

Sheridan, James E. 1966. *Chinese Warlord: The Career of Feng Yu-hsiang.* Stanford: Stanford University Press.

Stigler, George J. 1971. "The Theory of Economic Regulation." *Bell Journal of Economics and Management Science* 2:3–21.

Stigler, George J. 1992. "Law or Economics?" *Journal of Law and Economics* 35(2):455–468.

Szalai, Erzsebet. 1991. "Integration of Special Interests into the Hungarian Economy." *Journal of Comparative Economics* 15:284–303.

Thompson, Earl, and Roger Faith. 1981. "A Pure Theory of Strategic Behavior and Social Institutions." *American Economic Review* 71(3):366–380.

Vanhanen, Tatu. 1989. "The Level of Democratization Related to Socioeconomic Variables in 147 States in 1980–85." *Scandinavian Political Studies* 12(2):95–127.

Vedder, Richard, and Lowell Galloway. 1986. "Rentseeking, Distributional Coalitions, Taxes, Relative Prices, and Economic Growth." *Public Choice* 51(1):93–100.

Weede, Erich. 1986. "Catch-Up, Distributional Coalitions and Government as Determinants of Growth and Decline in Industrial Democracies." *British Journal of Sociology* 37:194–220.

Williamson, Oliver. 1985. *The Economic Institutions of Capitalism.* New York: The Free Press.

Winiecki, Jan. 1990. "Why Economic Reforms Fail in the Soviet System." *Economic Inquiry* 28:195–221.

Wittman, Donald. 1989. "Why Democracies Produce Efficient Results." *Journal of Political Economy* 97(6):1395–1424.

INDEX